UNDER THE RISING SUN

Memories of a
Japanese Prisoner of War

By Mario Machi

with an Introduction by Harold Stephens

Printed in Singapore.

ISBN: 0-9642521-0-4

Majority of photos appear
courtesy of:
The Arthur McBain Collection

Published by:

Wolfenden

U.S.A.
P.O. Box 789
Miranda, CA 95553-0789
Tel: (707) 923-2455 Fax: (707) 943-3955

SINGAPORE
Blk. 28 Kallang Place #03-16/17
Singapore 1233
Tel: (65) 294-4101 Fax: (65) 294-0515

"Brutality in war is as ancient as is warfare itself. But the Bataan death march lives in the chronicles of World War II as a sustained atrocity whose savagery revealed the character of the enemy—the attitude of his Army toward captives taken in battle— and shocked the American public...."

Lt. Col. William Dyess,
USA, Readers Digest

Acknowledgments

I want to give thanks to my wife, Shirley, and to all my family, who have been a great inspiration in my telling my story. I also want to thank Dr. Donald and Charlotte Pehlke, good friends, who have been wonderful in helping me to compile and complete this book. I owe them my gratitude.

And I want to thank Harold Stephens who encouraged me to republish and has so helpfully suggested making additions to the original text. He has also been kind enough to write the introduction for this edition.

There are others I would like to thank, but I know they are long gone, like the many Filipinos who risked their lives to smuggle food to us, and to the unforgotten man whom at the risk of his own life safeguarded my diary and returned it to me after the war had ended. And to so many more. God bless them, one and all.

General Joseph Stilwell Awards Corporal Mario Machi the Bronze Star for the work he had done with the sick and disabled prisoners in camp.

CONTENTS

IMPORTANT DATES

1940

Sept. 27 : Japan joins the Rome-Berlin Axis in the
Tripartite Pact for mutual defense.

1941

Feb. 17 : Mario Machi enlists as a private in the U.S. Army

July 10 : First American enlisted troops sent to the
Philippines

July 26 : President Roosevelt orders freezing Japanese
assets in the United States and discontinuing
trade with Japan.

Oct. 17 : General Hideki Tojo, war minister and leader
of military extremists, becomes Prime Minister
of Japan.

Oct. 23 : Pvt. Machi arrives in Manila aboard Tasker H.
Bliss

Nov. 14 : Saburo Kurusu, special envoy from Tokyo,
arrives in the United States to discuss the
Japanese-American crisis.

Dec. 7 : At 7:55 a.m. (Hawaiian time), Japan unleashes
surprise air attack on Pearl Harbor, imposing
immense damage on U.S. naval and military
forces. Tokyo declares war on the United States
and Britain.

Dec. 8 : U.S. Congress adopts declaration of war against
Japan; Churchill informs Parliament that
Britain is at war with Japan. Japanese forces
invade Thailand and Malaya. Japan makes first
landings and massive air attacks on Philippines.
Defending forces are under command of Gen.
Douglas MacArthur.

Dec. 25 : British colony of Hong Kong surrenders to
Japan.
Last boat leaves Manila for Bataan with Pvt.
Machi aboard.

1942

Jan.   2 :   Japanese take over Manila, as MacArthur's forces retire to Bataan Peninsula.

Jan.   11 :   Japanese invade Netherlands East Indies.

Feb.   15 :   Gen. Tomoyuki Yamashita receives the surrender of Singapore from British Gen. Arthur E. Percival.

Mar   1 :   Small Allied fleet under Dutch command destroyed in Battle of the Java Sea south of Philippines.

Mar   7 :   British evacuate Rangoon, capital of Burma.

Mar   11 :   Under orders from the President of the U.S., Gen. MacArthur leaves Corregidor aboard PT-41 for Australia

Apr   9 :   U.S. forces on Bataan surrender to Japanese. General Jonathan M. Wainwright retreats to Corregidor with small group.

Apr   10 :   Bataan Death March begins.

Apr   18 :   U.S. Army planes, commanded by Col. James H. Doolittle, carry out bombing raid on Tokyo.

Apr   29 :   Twenty days after their surrender, surviving prisoners of the Death March arrived at the rail junction at San Fernando, after having marched fifty-five miles on foot, leaving behind some 10,000 dead behind.

May   6 :   Gen. Wainwright surrenders Corregidor to the Japanese.

Jun   2 :   Prisoners of war transferred from Camp O'Donnell to Camp Cabanatuan north of Manila.

1943

Mar 2-4 :   Battle of the Bismarck Sea fought off the New Guinea coast; large portion of Japanese fleet destroyed.

1944

Feb. 21 :   Hideki Tojo, named chief of Japanese Army General Staff, becomes military dictator.

Apr	22 :	MacArthur leads landings in New Guinea.
Jun	15 :	U.S. Super Fortresses make first raids on Japan.
Jun	19 :	Carrier-borne U.S. aircraft attack the Japanese fleet between Luzon in Philippines and the Marianas, in the Battle of the Philippine Sea.
Jun	21 :	Okinawa falls to Americans.
July	21 :	U.S. marines and infantry establish beachheads on Guam.
Oct.	20 :	U.S. forces land on Leyte, in central Philippines.
Oct.	23 : to 26	Battle of Leyte Gulf; Japanese fleet suffers heavy losses.
Nov.	24 :	U.S. B-29's, based on Saipan, bomb Tokyo.

1945

Jan.	9 :	MacArthur's forces land on Luzon at Lingayen Gulf, 100 miles north of Manila.
Feb.	3 :	U.S. troops enter Manila.
Feb.	4 :	All American prisoners evacuated from Bilibid Prison.
Mar	9 :	Biggest B-29 bombing of Tokyo flattens sixteen square miles of city and kills 100,000.
Mar	15 :	*USS Monterey* arrives in San Francisco with Pvt, Machi and nearly 2,000 other ex-prisoners of war aboard.
Apr	1 :	American forces invade Okinawa, 340 miles south of Japan.
Apr	7 :	Baron Kantaro Suzuki becomes Japan's Prime Minister in shake-up.
May	3 :	Rangoon, Burma port, recaptured by British.
July	4 :	Gen. MacArthur announces liberation of the Philippines.
Aug	6 :	U.S. atom bomb is dropped on Hiroshima, virtually wiping out the Japanese city.
Aug	9 :	Atom bomb is dropped on Nagasaki, Japan.
Aug	14 :	Japan surrenders unconditionally; Emperor Hirohito announces defeat to his people.

Sept	2 :	Japanese Foreign Minister Mamoru Shigemitsu and military leaders sign surrender terms on the *U.S.S. Missouri* in Tokyo Bay.
Sept	15 :	Mario Machi discharged from the U.S. Army.

1980

Apr	5 :	Mario Machi, his wife Shirley and their two daughters depart San Francisco International Airport for Manila.
Apr	9 :	The survivors of the Bataan Death march stand at the foot of a huge cross on top of Mount Samat on the Bataan Peninsula. Mario Machi and his family stand with them.

INTRODUCTION

Harold Mendes is a business man, born and raised in northern California, and he knows just about everyone and anyone who lives in Humboldt County. If he doesn't know them personally, he knows all about them. It wasn't long after I got to know him that he told me about Mario Machi. "You've got to meet him. He's a writer, like yourself," he said. "He was a prisoner-of-war, you know." Then he added, "He lives in Shelter Cove, has a marina there."

I usually don't fancy meeting writers "like myself" and probably would have declined his offer had I not been anxious to visit Shelter Cove. I was new to redwood country and had heard about the merits of this beautiful hidden cove tucked away on the Pacific Coast.

We made the 24-mile drive one Sunday afternoon and found Mario talking to a couple of boat owners in front of his marina overlooking the cove. A dozen boats were at anchor, waiting to be pulled ashore; others were entering the harbor.

Mario greeted us warmly and we shook hands. He was soft spoken and easy-mannered. He was past 70 then, a bit stocky, suntanned and obviously very fit for his age. His hair was white and he had a neatly trimmed moustache. He sported a well-worn captain's hat with an anchor emblem at the peak. In a conversation that was all too brief (more pleasure boats with their salmon catches were coming in), he mentioned something about serving in the Philippines and that he had a great admiration for the Filipinos, but he spoke mostly about the cove and the fishing season not being what it used to be.

Other bits of information about Mario had come from Harold Mendes on our drive down to the cove. It seems that after Mario was discharged from the army, he completed college and then taught school for twenty-two years at an elementary and junior high school in Miranda, a small town in northern California. Later I met another teacher, Rip Kirby, who had taught school in Miranda the same time as Mario did. "Mario was the hardest working man I had ever met," Rip said when I asked him about Mario. "He drove a school bus in the morning, taught school all day and then in the evening ran the Grotto Restaurant in Redway. He did the cooking as well. He's a man that just can't be idle."

Mario had acquired some land in Shelter Cove and when he had the capital he developed it. Mario's Marina is one of the biggest and most prosperous enterprises in Shelter Cove today.

As I was leaving Shelter Cove that first time, Mario thanked me for stopping by, and as I was getting into the car he handed me a book, a small book less than a hundred pages, titled *The Emperor's Hostages*. His name appeared below the title. "It's one of my last copies," he said. "You might want to read it."

I began reading the book the very next day. Once I started, I couldn't do another thing until I finished it. As I read I kept picturing Mario, standing at the Marina in Shelter Cove, a proud successful man, and then I saw the same man, almost fifty years before, being kicked and savagely beaten, forced to march through malaria infested jungles for nearly sixty miles with neither food nor water to drink. And I could see marching side by side with him other prisoners, men too weak to continue, dropping by the roadside, only to be bayoneted for failing to keep up. Somehow Mario managed to survive the brutality, the hunger, the thirst, the disease, and the dreadful feeling that he had been abandoned. Some 10,000 men died on that march, an average of 178 men for every mile they tread. But Mario Machi lived.

I wanted desperately to talk to Mario again; there was so much to ask him. I couldn't help wondering about the many people who had read *The Emperor's Hostages*, his students, the fishermen who used the marina, even his fiends, how many of them knew anything about Mario the prisoner-of-war, a soldier who had survived the notorious Bataan Death March? How can one equate Mario the soldier with Mario the devoted husband and father, the school teacher, the man who runs the marina in Shelter Cove?

I can't remember but I may have seen Mario a half dozen times after that, at the bank in Garberville, and at the Cove when I took friends down to visit. Each time I saw him I thought about the war in the Pacific. Always in the back of my mind was the hope that one day I might be able to sit down with him and ask about those days of long ago. But I didn't. The days passed, the months and the years.

Then, on May 6, 1992, an event took place that left an impression so deep I won't ever be able to forget it. And it was at that moment that Mario's book took on a new meaning and came to life for me.

On that day in the heat of the afternoon, with eighty former prisoners-of-war, I entered Malinta Tunnel on the island of Corregidor in the Philippines. As a journalist, I was invited by the Philippine government to attend a ceremony marking the 50th anniversary of the Fall of Corregidor. The Corregidor Foundation was staging a light-and-sound presentation of the siege of Corregidor that they called "The Malinta Experience."

As we stood there inside the tunnel, not knowing what to expect, the lights dimmed and then went out. We were in total darkness. Suddenly this was not May 6, 1992, but May 6, 1942.

From somewhere deep in the tunnel a bomb blast ended our silence. It was followed by another, and another. Shock after shock vibrated through the rock walls! A string of light bulbs suspended from the ceiling came on, dimly, flickering, swinging from side to side. The concrete floor beneath our feet trembled with such violence I reached for something to grab. Soon the sound was deafening, like a weight pressing down, about to crush us. Dust fell from everywhere and the walls seemed as though they might collapsed.

The godawful feeling, the sensation we encountered, was about as close as we could get to the real thing. In fact, it was so realistic I wanted to break loose from the others and run from the tunnel. Any of us could very easily have done that, run for the light at the far end, but for the soldiers who were defending the rock fifty years ago that would have been impossible. They were doomed to die, or else surrender to the Japanese.

On May 6, 1942, after defending the island fortress for five long months, General Jonathan Wainwright did just that—surrender. He gave the orders to raise a white flag. Corregidor had fallen.

Following the presentation I stood on Corregidor with a half dozen former prisoners and looked across the water toward Bataan. The peninsula appeared peaceful and serene, like a color photograph in a travel magazine. But the men who stood beside me remembered another Bataan. And it was then, standing there on Corregidor, that I remembered Mario Machi and his book.

Corregidor was only half the story of what had happened to American forces in the Philippines. The other half, what took place on the Peninsula of Bataan, was Mario Machi's story, and I knew then that I had to talk to him again. The story he told in *The Emperor's Hostages* was all too brief. I read through the text again, and came up with hundreds of unanswered questions. I wanted to know more about Manila and the Philippines, and, of course, more about the Japanese. Why did these men, the prisoners as well as the Japanese guards, act the way they did? The story that Mario has to tell the world is history in its purest sense. It's not history told by a scholar who gets his information from research but by one who had been there, one who had seen and witnessed it first hand,

and who had recorded in a diary many events as they were happening. And most miraculously, this leather-bound diary—a written confession that would certainly have meant immediate death to Mario had it fallen into enemy hands—has survived to this day. Mario's story is a story for this generation and for future generations to read and ponder. Then, perhaps, we might better understand what went wrong with the world back in 1941, and hopefully learn from those mistakes.

I finally met with Mario, now nearing eighty years old, in Shelter Cove, and he was receptive to my suggestion that he republish his memoirs. When we did sit down together to discuss the new book, often with his wife Shirley present, I was surprised to find he could recall with minute accuracy every detail of his war years experiences. And Shirley added greatly to his story. She could relate the more intimate details, about death and suffering, and about loving too, that Mario had revealed to her in their years together.

Sometimes when talking to Mario our conversations took painful twists. Mario's eyes occasionally filled with tears as he recalled a particularly painful incident. At other times he corrected my assumptions. I remember saying to him, "You really had to be a wheeler-dealer to survive." In a stern voice he fired back, "I survived because I was not a wheeler-dealer."

Mario immediately set to work on the revision with the new title *Under the Rising Sun.* He has expanded the original text and answered many questions that had gone unanswered. Some questions, however, cannot be answered, and it is up the reader to find his own interpretations.

Under the Rising Sun is written for both the generations who remember Bataan and for those who have yet to hear. It is the story of survival under conditions of utmost brutality and depravation, but more importantly it stands as witness to the values that sustained the author on his terrible journey: his sense of humor, his love for country, family and friends, and finally his commitment to work and to helping those whose circumstances were even worse than his. On his return to the United States in 1945, Mario Machi was awarded the Bronze Star for the work he had done in the camps. Now, a half century later, he has told his story, and we are all made the richer for it.

Readers will notice some chapters contain headings in italics. Most of these are historical notes that I prepared and are not necessarily the opinion nor the conclusion of the author. I have added them in hope that they serve to enlighten readers to other events that were happening at the time. It is impossible to set all the facts straight. For example, every history text and every source material lists a different number for prisoners lost during the death march. Some sources believe the figure is well over 10,000. But such figures and facts are not what concerns Mario Machi. He leaves that to the writers of text books.

Harold Stephens
California, June 1994

PREMONITION

I lay on the deck,
The cool steel under my neck,
The stars above, the sea below,
The ship rocking to and fro,

As the ship goes forward,
My thoughts turn homeward,
To the mischievous ways
Of my boyhood days.

Fate has now taken the helm,
Steering us into an unknown realm.
Death lurks high on the mast,
Waiting for a die to be cast...

Mario Machi,
October 18, 1941, aboard ship
en route to the Philippines.

THE CALL TO ARMS

"Never in American history was an event more anticipated yet more of a surprise than the attack on Pearl Harbor,".... Time Magazine.

Against my father's advice, I dropped out of college and enlisted in the Army of the United States of America on February 17, 1941 at Letterman General Hospital in San Francisco. Like most everyone in America in early 1941, I thought war in the Pacific was imminent and I believed it would be best for me to enlist early and get myself into something I liked. I had three years of college behind me, at San Francisco State, with a major in physical education. I had studied anatomy and biology and some medicine and decided the medical corps might be the answer.

Unfortunately, I received very little training and in September of the same year I asked for a transfer to the infantry. During this time I met men with whom I would serve in Manila and then later on Bataan. I got my request, and never was a transfer so immediate, and for good reason. No sooner had I joined my new outfit than we received orders to move out. We were going to the Philippine Islands across the Pacific.

On September 26 we transferred from Letterman to Fort McDowell and a week later on October 4 we sailed for the islands. During this week I truly enjoyed my last look at San Francisco, my home town. In the evenings with a couple buddies I would walk up to the summit above the fort where beneath a full moon I could look out over the town, the Golden Gate Bridge and Alcatraz, and to as far away as other cities on the bay. The weather much of that week was warm and clear and lovely. I made a dollar on a bet when Joe Louis floored Nova.

One day two friends and I got passes to the city. We

enjoyed abalone sandwiches on Fisherman's Wharf, a banana split in North Beach and then had dinner with my family. My whole family had not been together like this for some months; it would be even longer before we were together again. That night on the way back to Fort McDowell my friends and I made wishes and for good luck each of us tossed pennies into the bay. I spoke my wish aloud and then later in the barracks I faithfully recorded it in my diary. I hoped that we would all have experiences of value in the islands and would return again to the U.S.A. Two months later when we were thrown into a world we had not thought humanly possible, those wishes would seem naive and far away.

Chapter 1

GOODBYE FRISCO,
HELLO SOUTH PACIFIC
———————•◆•———————

Since 1936, American military officers had been serving in the Philippines, organizing and training Filipino troops. When the threat of war in the Pacific increased, the Philippine Army was ordered into the regular service of the U.S. Army. Finally in July, 1941, American enlisted troops were sent to the Philippines to further assist with the training of Filipinos and to prepare for the defense of the islands. Mario Machi was among those sent to the Philippines...HS

At 2:30 p.m. we boarded *Tasker H. Bliss*, formerly *President Cleveland*, a grand old luxury liner that had seen better and happier days. Gone were its luster and polish; it was now repainted and converted into a troop transport that carried 5,000 officers and men, crammed into tight quarters with pipe bunk beds stacked eight high. Our quarters were aft about three flights down in a converted freight hold. Sailing with us was *Williard A. Holbrook*, formerly *President Taft*, another converted liner bearing the same dismal grey color. A band played "Anchors Away" and a large crowd gathered on the dock shouting and waving to wish well and to send us on our way. Some men threw their garrison caps to the pretty girls on shore. We left at 5:30 that afternoon and the two ships sailed together through the Golden Gate and embarked for Hawaii, our first stop en route to the Philippines.

An hour after we left the Golden Gate we encountered rough seas and a strong wind out of the northwest. Soon most of the men were heaving over the railing. I did not feel so good myself but I was fortunate that I didn't have to heave like the others.

Seeing the others did remind me of my first voyage on the open sea. It had been aboard a drag boat out of San Francisco for Shelter Cove along the northern California coast. Due to bad weather, what would normally have been a seventeen hour voyage, took us twenty-four. Before leaving the dock in San Francisco, we had each eaten a bowl of the captain's salmon soup, and although I had followed a friend's suggestion and nibbled on soda crackers and chewed a lemon, I became deathly seasick before we passed through the Golden Gate. The sickness remained with me throughout the trip, and it wasn't until I had been ashore for some time that I felt normal again. To this day I can taste the salmon soup that nauseated me then.

Now, as I watched my sick comrades aboard the *Bliss*, I remembered how weak and wobbly I had been as I climbed up the ladder and stood on the pier at Shelter Cove that beautiful day. I can still recall the exact date, May 22, 1930. The boat that brought us was owned by the San Francisco International Fish Company, a company my father, Pietro Machi, helped start back in 1908. He was still a stockholder then in the company.

Although I was only sixteen at the time, I was deeply impressed with Shelter Cove. As I studied the rugged coastline and the cove itself, I marveled at the spectacular scenery. I even thought how fine it would be to have a seaside resort there one day.

The trip to Honolulu took five days. Every day I played my accordion, usually on deck beneath the shade of a life boat, and often with a trumpet player I met on board. Some days we had work assignments, chipping paint and scrubbing the decks. We saw flying fish and had our first blackout, which lasted twenty minutes. The weather was balmy and so hot in the holds we were forced to sleep without blankets or clothes.

It was October 9th, my birthday, that *Tasker H. Bliss* rounded the southeastern tip of Oahu in the Hawaiian Islands and Diamond Head came into view. Soldiers crowded the railing and joked about seeing coconuts, pineapples and hula girls. In the distance five or six planes circled in the sky. We entered a narrow channel that opened up into a wide port as big as a lake. All about we could see powerful battle wagons, destroyers and their escorts and a couple of carriers either at anchor and or else moored along the docks. The sailors aboard who had been here before called the place Pearl Harbor. "A good liberty port," they told us. Some asked if the name comes because there are pearls in the harbor. With excitement we talked about our shore leave. We were assured of leave and each man had dressed in his cleanest suntan outfit, ready to rush down the gangplank the moment we docked.

As we came along side the dock, a band started playing and we could see hula girls dancing on the pier. We were excited beyond words. Our first port-of-call. But when a destroyer came and tied up along side us, I sensed something was wrong. And sure enough I was right, for as we lined the deck, waiting for the gangplank to be lowered, a voice came over the loudspeaker. It was the commanding officer. He announced that no one was to leave the ship. Our sailing time had been set for 5:00 the following morning.

The men were terribly disappointed. They voiced their disapproval by grumbling and making nasty remarks. The band stopped playing, the hula girls disappeared and a cordon of M.P.s now lined the dock. The order was meant to be enforced. This was as close as I ever came to the Hawaiian Islands.

Chapter 2

RED SAILS IN
THE SUNSET

I was up at the crack of dawn and on deck when we cast off our mooring lines and headed back out to sea. I saw the name of the destroyer as it took up a position in the lead as escort vessel—*USS Chester.* I was more interested in the view of the island than I was of the ships in the harbor. In the back of our minds we knew that here was the mightiest navy in the world and no power on earth could ever do it harm. We believed it, as everyone back home in America did. Foremost in our thoughts was the anger at being denied shore leave. Breakfast was delayed that morning for there were no volunteers for K.P. Why, we wondered, couldn't they have let us go ashore? There wasn't a war going on!

The two troop ships took up positions side by side with the destroyer sailing between and slightly in front of us. After dinner that first night out of Honolulu we were given orders that called for a complete blackout each night. We were also given permission to sleep on deck. It rained a little during the night but I didn't mind. It was cool and the moon on the water was beautiful.

The next day, to break the monotony, I let my friends shave my head. We had fun and I took much razzing but I didn't mind. When we didn't have work details, we spent our time gambling and playing cards while some wrestled and frolicked on deck. One day while on work detail I found an old cot. I bragged about how wonderful it would be to sleep on deck with a cot. But that night when I set it up and stretched out it collapsed with a bang on the hard steel deck, to everyone's laughter. I discovered the cot was beyond repair and pitched it in the rubbish. I ended up sleeping in the hold with the rest of the men. My bragging had cost me some teasing for a long time to come. Another night after supper Sergeant Sayer and I went to the officers' social hall to play music for a colonel's birthday party. The sergeant pounded away at the piano while I played the accordion. I became disgusted when I saw the luxury the officers enjoyed compared to the life we enlisted men had to lead in the hell hole where we slept.

We crossed the International Date Line and dropped south across the Equator and paid our dues to Neptune, a shipmate with a mop for a hairdo and a toilet plunger for a scepter. The nights were complete blackouts with not even cigarette smoking permitted above deck. It was miserable below deck. The heat and smell in the holds were dreadful. We slept on deck whenever possible. But almost without fail it rained and we had to grab our bedding and rush below.

The mornings were usually beautiful and the days balmy, and the ocean a magnificent purplish blue. We never tired of watching flying fish break the surface and shoot across our bow. We marveled how far some could fly, floating only inches above the surface of the water, only to disappear beyond the crest of a breaking wave. We also wondered what monstrous fish might be chasing them to send them flipping across the water as they did. A song I was requested to play on my accordion every day was "Red Sails in the Sunset." Sometimes Jake the trumpeter accompanied me and half a dozen men kept the beat on tin cans and boxes.

Early the morning of October 19 we sighted a verdant, high volcanic island. Word came down the line that it was Guam, one of America's eastern naval bases. It was raining and there was a rainbow in the sky. The officers and non-coms were allowed shore leave but the rest of us were not. At six-thirty that evening, while the enlisted men grumbled, we pulled away from the island and sailed westward.

The rest of the trip to the Philippines was uneventful, except now below the Equator dreamy days and balmy evenings were interspersed with rain squalls, crashing thunder and a sky filled with flashes of lightning. It was especially awesome to come on deck at night, into pitch blackness, and suddenly see both sky and sea light up from one horizon to the other in a single flash.

We continued to spend much time watching flying fish jump in front of the bow, and now in the warmer tropical waters of the South Pacific came another marvel— an ocean that glowed, like a sky that's lighted with billions of fireflies. At first the phenomena appeared to be reflections from the stars as we cut a course through the water, but we soon learned that on moonlit nights the plankton-rich seas of the South Pacific glow with phosphorus. They were like diamonds you wanted to reach out and grab.

Four days after leaving Guam we sighted the Philippine Islands and by evening we were sailing through the San Bernardine Strait, the narrow channel that separates Luzon in the north from the twin islands of Samar and Leyte in the south. "We all crowded the rails, and there was quite a bit of excitement," I wrote in my diary. "We are now heading into the most beautiful sunset I have ever seen. The ocean is just like a lake with hardly a ripple on the water."

Once through the channel, we turned north and entered the Visayan Sea. I slept on deck and was up at 4:30 and began writing in my diary: "Awoke during the night to see islands on both sides of the ship, and this morning there are islands in every direction. On the starboard side there is a mountainous island that resembles a volcano. The peak is shrouded in clouds and it's actually hard to tell what it is. All the islands are quite close and we can see vegetation. The water is calm although there is a fresh breeze blowing. All the boys are on deck and we are getting quite a kick out of the flying fish. Coconuts and strange sea kelp float by. At 9:20 a.m. two U.S. Army pursuit planes dove at us, over and over, giving us a show. It was quite thrilling."

In a few weeks seeing planes dive at us would no longer be a thrill. It would turn to terror.

We sailed into beautiful Manila Bay, where the rock of Corregidor, like a lone sentinel, guarded the entrance as it had done diligently for the Spanish for 400 years before the Americans came.

At last, we were in Manila, the end of our journey. *Tasker H. Bliss* and *Williard A. Holbrook* ended their voyage at the docks at Cavite on October 23. To mark our arrival, a rainbow above the city was there to greet us. We tied up to the dock and excitedly disembarked with all our gear to a wonderful reception. There was a strong sense of patriotism in the air. I felt I now knew that proud feeling the Yanks had experienced when they landed in Europe during the First World War. A band played the Philippine and American national anthems while Filipino stevedores sold bottles of cokes for a quarter and packs of cigarettes for a dime. We boarded Army trucks and through cheering crowds drove to Fort McKinley. Here we were assigned to our new units.

After having lived in San Francisco all my life, I now witnessed sights in Manila that both amazed and baffled me. If I had only one word to describe the scene that unfolded before us as we drove through the streets that first evening, it would be "crazy." Manila was, indeed, a crazy yet beautiful city. Most striking was Intramuros, the Walled City, the show piece of Manila. Built by the Spanish in the 16th century, it had walls sixteen feet high and forty feet thick at the base, tapering to twenty feet at the top. Watch towers stood at all the corners, and massive wooden gates with carved lintels faced the four points of the compass.

And never had any of us seen traffic like they had in Manila in those days. Little ponies with tinkling bells pulled painted, two-wheel carriages, and colorful taxis blew their horns incessantly, taxis with so many decorations on their bumpers, fenders and hoods their driver could hardly see through the windshields. Two-wheeled wagons were loaded so heavily with boxes and crates that each time they hit a rut, which was often, the ponies' hooves raised up from the cobblestone streets. Every now and then a water buffalo—they called them carabaos—pulling a load of bagged rice would slowly amble up the street, blocking traffic even more.

And to add to the confusion, all traffic—buses, cars, taxis, bicycles, horse carriages, carabaos pulling carts— they all moved ahead on the left side of the road like traffic does in England.

To us it appeared that Manila's population could not possibly get anywhere through the din and confusion of their traffic and congestion, yet strange as it seemed, the vehicles kept moving.

It was, however, the people, the Filipinos and the Filipinas, that more than anything else caught our attention. Both men and women wore native dress. The women looked lovely in their colorful long skirts and fancy cotton blouses; the men wore baggy trousers and sandals. Everyone, man, woman and child, stopped to cheer us as we drove past. From the very start I knew I would like the Filipinos.

At Fort McKinley I received my assignment. I was attached to Sternberg General hospital to work in the physiotherapy clinic. My college training was paying off.

The month of November came and went. Usually I worked in the morning and then had the rest of the day to myself. My instructor on the ward was a nurse, Miss Kuethahl. My work consisted mostly of applying heat lamps to injured or strained muscles. During my free time I went strolling through the streets of Manila. There were endless sights to see and things to do. It was a pleasant month and no one really gave much thought to the possibility of war with Japan. In the upper echelon it may have been different, but in the ranks I don't think any of us thought it would happen, though there was some preparation. One night a practice blackout was ordered for Manila. Another time we had a gas mask drill. The Filipinos we came to know seemed the least worried. The United States Army was there now to protect them. All would be well.

I enjoyed my free time in Manila more than anything. In the evenings I took my accordion with me into town, and in the barrios I sat with the people and played for them. They loved it. The Filipinos were happy-go-lucky and they seemed to love our being there. They made us feel wanted.

Other times we went to the bars. There was music everywhere and every night was exciting. Sometimes I would stroll along the paths outside the Walled City. But I had to be very careful. People who lived in quarters facing the wall often threw their rubbish out the windows, and more than once I had to be quick and duck out of the way to miss a bucket load of trash, or whatever it might be.

But black clouds were gathering. The good days in Manila were soon to end, abruptly and without warning. The date was December 8, 1941; the time, early morning.

The day began like every other day for us in the Philippines. We lined up outside our barracks for roll call and afterward the sergeant-in-charge set us to work policing the area—picking up cigarette butts and bits of papers. The news that Pearl Harbor was bombed a few hours before was kept from us. To this day I will never understand why the command didn't tell us. When one man from headquarters came along and whispered what had happen, I laughed. It was only rumor, I thought. The Japanese, the makers of cheap toys and kid's firecrackers, wouldn't dare bomb America. It would be suicide.

But then more rumors came. Now word spread through the hospital that Guam, too, had been struck, and also Clark Field to the north of us.

Finally it was announced. We were in a state of war with Japan and were given our first orders, to go get our gas masks. For us in the Philippines it may have been Monday morning, but for Hawaii in a different time zone it was a still Sunday, a little past noon, on that infamous date—December 7th.

What we were later to learn was that a Japanese naval striking force—with two battleships, two heavy cruisers, eleven destroyers and six big aircraft carriers carrying 423 planes—had assembled 275 miles north of Oahu in the Hawaiian Islands and without announcing a declaration of war bombed Pearl Harbor. At 7:55 a.m. that Sunday morning, while we were at roll call, the bombs began to fall at Pearl. When it ended about two hours later, the toll was fearsome. Some 2,403 soldiers, sailors, marines and civilians were dead, and 1,178 more wounded. Eighteen ships were sunk or seriously damaged, and 149 planes were destroyed on the ground. The mighty *USS Arizona* that we had seen at anchor at Pearl Harbor only three short months before, was rolled over with 1,120 men trapped inside. In all, 1,177 sailors and marines had lost their lives aboard that ship.

The Japanese lost but 29 planes.

Outside the hospital the streets were bedlam.

Everyone was looking up at the sky. At three in the afternoon I was ordered to throw all my gear in a barracks bag and get ready. We were told we were going to Fort Stotsenberg and Clark Field. We didn't know when we would be returning. I had to leave my accordion with a friend in the barracks and I could only hope it would be there when I returned.

As we passed through the streets of Manila, I could see confused Filipinos standing on the pavements looking up at the sky, waiting, wondering. Suddenly our convoy of trucks and jeeps came to an abrupt halt. Six Japanese fighter planes came swooping over the city and flew directly over our heads. Everyone was too dumfounded even to run for cover. How wrong we had been. The Japanese were attacking. There was no mistaking now. This was not rumors. It was real. We were being attacked. The premonition I had back in the States was right. War had arrived in the Pacific.

Chapter 3

THE ENEMY OVERHEAD

———◆———

Early on the morning of December 8th, only a few short hours after they began dropping bombs on Pearl Harbor, the Japanese struck the Philippines. By the end of the first day the U.S. Army Air Forces had lost more than half its bombers and a third of its fighter planes based there. The major Japanese assault was at Clark Air Base. Then two days later, during the early morning of December 10th, practically the entire Navy yard at Cavite was destroyed by enemy bombers. The first Japanese landings took place that same day on Luzon north of Manila, and so began the invasion of the Philippine islands... HS

Soldiers in the field, the fighting men, know little about what is going on beyond their own line of defense. All they can see, and know, is what is happening directly in front of them. This was the case with us. We drove into the night through a blackout and were often delayed by stalled trucks that had been pushed aside into the ditches. We reached our destination but found the hospital in chaos. Doctors and nurses had been up all night tending the causalities. Sixty soldiers lay dead and another hundred were injured from the bombings. I was sent to work in the dressing room, and found myself giving blood when a doctor called for a transfusion and there was no one around to help. When I did get to bed, it was after midnight, and shortly after, at 2:15 am, I experienced my first air raid. Fortunately no bombs hit the hospital.

In the morning I volunteered to help pull bodies, and parts of bodies, out of the wreckage and lay the remains in the open in hope they could be recognized. It was a pitiful sight. Tearful Filipinos moved among the remains attempting to identify members of their families. Most of the dead could not be identified. Some bodies had been burned to a crisp. One man in tattered clothing, himself suffering from shock, searched for two brothers, a sister and his mother and father. When I left the site a few hours later, he was still searching. This was the morning that I was introduced to the horrors of war. I made the following entry in my diary:

"I always wanted action and new experiences. I think I have had enough now. This is horrible. I am gazing out across the athletic field. The scenery is peaceful and beautiful. What a shame that the poor soldiers I moved this morning cannot be alive and happy and at peace with the world."

I was assigned to Ward 5 at the air base hospital located next to the airfield. I was no sooner posted to my ward when the bombing began again. We hurriedly put the patients on stretchers and carried them out of the ward and placed them beneath the building.

It was around noon of the 10th that we received word that Japanese paratroopers had landed and were advancing toward the air field. Tanks were immediately deployed around the area and we were led to believe the attack could come at any minute. The order came for us to evacuate all patients to Manila by rail. It seemed like an impossible task but we grabbed every available vehicle and somehow managed to transport most of the patients to the railhead. We then returned to the wards to care for the remaining patients who were too weak to move and awaited an uncertain fate. But the Japanese ground troops did not arrive as expected.

On December 12th I wrote in my diary: "No air raid last night. Had a good sleep. Went to work in Ward 5. At 11:15 am I was working under the ward preparing beds for air raids. The day was cloudy and it was raining.

Suddenly without warning the Japs hit us with bombs. Three flights of bombers swooped over at 500 feet and dropped bombs all around us. I shoved my face in the dirt, said my prayers, and just waited. I saw one bomb go off about 100 yards from where I lay. The ground was shaking. Boy, ole boy, ole boy, what a feeling! Causalities are now coming into the hospital. I can see them from the window of the ward. They are coming from all directions."

On the 13th we were bombed at 7:30, 8:15 and 10:30, all in the morning. Before noon we received another air raid warning and I wrote: "I wish to say that it has been a miracle that this hospital hasn't been hit as yet. God help us if it is."

During most of these raids there was little opportunity to move the patients below. I couldn't leave them. Instead I sat between two patients and held their hands while the bombs dropped around us. We talked about our planes coming to our rescue, but deep down none of us really believed they would. We had seen the destroyed planes at the base.

Soon the bombing became so heavy, so intense, that we felt we might fall apart. Our nerves were about to break. Any unusual noise would send us scurrying for cover under the mess hall tables. At one meal the mess sergeant had an announcement he intended to read for the company, but it was impossible for him to get their attention. I suggested he blow the whistle he had hanging on a cord around his neck. I was standing next to him when he gave a shrill blast on the whistle, which, unfortunately, sounded somewhat like a bomb on its way down. Pandemonium suddenly broke out as everyone in the hall dashed for an exit. Men jumped over tables, falling and stumbling over one another as they searched for cover. Dishes flew in all directions. A cook dropped a large pot, spilling the boiling contents across the floor. Another man threw his crutches aside and dove through an open window. In much less than one minute, the mess hall was empty except for me and the mess sergeant. He still held the paper that he had intended to read. He stood looking at the empty hall with an expression of disbelief on his face. I slipped away from him as quietly as I could.

Over the next few days we evacuated the remaining patients to Manila. When the last of them were placed aboard the flatcars, we returned to the wards and straightened up the area. We had a post telephone set up under the steps of the ward, and that evening I was detailed to man the phone. Sitting there surrounded by sandbags and waiting for the phone to ring that would announce another air raid, I suddenly heard the sound of women singing. It seemed incomprehensible. Then I realized what it was. I was hearing the voices of nurses who were quartered underneath the ward father down the line. They were singing "Oh Holy Night," and I remembered now that it was close to Christmas, and we were far, far from home.

The next few days were more quiet. We spent the time digging bomb shelters outside the hospital. All the work was done by hand, with pick axes and shovels. Laboring in the hot sun was exhausting. We were also detailed to cover the windows of the buildings with tar paper. A rumor spread during the lull that our planes had bombed the Japanese air base and their planes were silenced. On Sunday the 21st we even played a game of baseball. Then on the 24th of December, the day before Christmas, we received sudden orders to evacuate the hospital and Clark Field. We heard the sad news that our defending troops in the north were steadily retreating. We had little time left. We were told the Japanese were two days from Clark Field.

We loaded all the hospital supplies we could aboard railroad flatcars and returned to Manila. As we approached the city we realized that the rumor that our planes had bombed the Japanese base was false. We could see thick black smoke pouring from the center of city. An air raid was in progress as we arrived. We witnessed a mass exodus of Manila; people carried what they could on their backs, while others pulled wagons and carts loaded down with their belongings. Ponies lay dead in their harnesses, and vehicles were abandoned in the streets where they had been strafed. Rubble of burned out buildings smouldered and sent out choking clouds of smoke. Japanese bombers flew freely over the city and bombed any target they wished. Manila was in complete chaos. The city was doomed.

On Christmas Day, we boarded trucks that transported us to Port Area for further evacuation. But to where? When we arrived at the port we looked for ships in the harbor, but there were none, except a single battered cargo ship tied to the dock. The name across her bow read *Carmen*. To our dismay we learned she was the one that was scheduled to take us to Bataan where Filipino and American troops were amassing for their final defense before help from America arrived. *Carmen* was our last hope.

Japanese Advancing during the drive on Manila.

Chapter 4

LAST BOAT TO BATAAN

———◦◆◦◦———

Stacked on the pier in front of the cargo ship were about forty heavy packing crates which we were instructed to load aboard before we left. We were about to begin when an air raid alarm sounded and within minutes enemy planes appeared from across the harbor. Everyone on deck and on the dock dropped whatever he was doing and made a mad dash for a trap door that led to a makeshift shelter below the pier. The entrance to the shelter became so plugged with soldiers shoving and pushing that not a single person could get through. The Japanese dive bombers dumped their first load of bombs alongside *Carmen*. Most bombs landed in the water, but a few did start fires abroad the ship.

The Manila Fire Department arrived after the planes left. I helped firefighters carry a hose aboard the ship, and when they were set I held firmly to the nozzle and waited. When water finally came it did so with such force it was all I could do to hang on to the hose. I looked around for help but everyone had disappeared. They were fleeing the hose that was now out of control. I shouted for assistance and little by little men scrambled one by one out of their hiding places.

The fires out, we were put to work again loading the packing crates aboard *Carmen*.

But no sooner were the crates aboard than the order came to put them back on the dock. Fires below deck had flared up. It took another half hour to unload the ship while we continued to fight the flames on board. Finally with the fires out, we received further orders to reload the crates. We couldn't believe it. Whatever the crates contained, it had to be valuable to risk the lives of the men and the ship. We cursed as we struggled up the narrow gangplank to get the crates back aboard.

We had just sat down on the deck for a well-deserved rest when the air raid siren sounded for the second time. Immediately bombs were falling and men were scrambling for cover. A few men leaped overboard. The Japanese had a clear shot at *Carmen* yet she took no direct hits. Apparently they did not want to sink her. They were only trying to disable her. Fires broke out again on deck. As soon as the raid was over, we were again ordered to take the crates off the ship. "What? Aren't things bad enough?" I heard someone shout, but the order stood firm. By now our cursing extended not only to the Japanese but to the officers in charge, the army, the packing crates and even the narrow gangplank.

After the fires had been put out, the captain determined that *Carmen* was capable of making the trip. For the last time we reloaded the crates. The men filed aboard and soon every bit of space above and below deck was occupied. Soldiers sat everywhere, atop the piles of cargo, along the rails with their feet hanging over the sides, even on the bridge. Hawsers were cast off and *Carmen* slowly moved away from the dock. Every last man was dead tired from the endless air raids and from loading and unloading the packing crates.

Japanese planes had been flying sorties over the bay all the morning, dropping bombs on installations and strafing the area, and here we were on the upper deck, wide open to aerial attack, without protection. We were apprehensive, watching for the slightest glare of an approaching enemy plane, but none appeared. The sky remained clear, but our ordeal was far from over. We were faced with another threat which could be even more foreboding than bombs and machine-gun fire. We might all drown in shark-infested water. *Carmen's* starboard hull at the waterline had been punctured during the air raids. She had gaping holes in her side and was taking on more water than her pumps could handle. We not only looked for planes now but for sharks as well. Then suddenly, as we were approaching the rocky Bataan shoreline, the vessel made a lung to the starboard, nearly knocking half of us overboard. At full steam the captain now headed *Carmen* straight for the beach. Before we knew what was happening she struck a sand bar and ran high aground. The captain had saved the day. The ship was safe, for the time being.

Before long a launch appeared, and for last time we unloaded the packing crates from *Carmen* to the launch. The launch then took us and our precious cargo ashore.

Once ashore we discovered we would have to remain over night on the beach, but we had no food. The captain remembered that *Carmen* still had a hefty supply of canned goods aboard. He asked for volunteers and a half dozen of us returned to the ship to get whatever supplies we could find. We climbed aboard and as the captain held a flashlight I descended the ladder into the hold. The captain was right; there were cases of canned food everywhere. I picked out about twenty cases of assorted canned goods, from hams to peaches, which we hauled on deck and then loaded on to the launch. We returned to the beach where a jubilant but hungry bunch of soldiers awaited us. The way we ate and clowned around one would not have thought the Japanese were just across the way. I wished I had my accordion.

We slept on the beach that night and early the next morning a convoy of trucks arrived to take us and our cargo to a command post in the jungle. One driver, obviously with little experience in driving trucks, was having a difficult time with his vehicle. I offered to take over, which he gladly agreed to. The truck was not much different from one I had driven one summer when I hauled frozen fish from Eureka in northern California down to San Francisco. What a contrast this was, from the redwoods of California to the jungle of Bataan. From frozen fish to god knows what.

The jungle post turned out to be Camp Lamaz, the medical headquarters for the Thirty-first Infantry Regiment. Doctors and nurses jumped with excitement when they saw us arrive with the packing crates. We didn't feel so bad now knowing all our efforts to save the crates were well deserved. The crates, no doubt, contained much needed medical supplies. Two enlisted men hastily broke open several boxes and before they could step back doctors and nurses rushed to the fore to take over. Our happiness turned to anger. The officers searched not for medical supplies but instead for their own personal belongings. We were shocked to see them pull from the crates tennis rackets and golf clubs, tuxedos and evening gowns. The memory of having moved these heavy boxes on and off *Carmen,* the sweat and labor involved, and the risk of both lives and ship, was fresh in our minds. The feelings we had at that time are unprintable. Later that day, when we were together and away from the officers, we mused at the thought of the Japanese pilots not wanting to sink *Carmen* thinking that her cargo was undoubtedly of great valuable to the war effort, and by merely disabling the ship the cargo would eventually be theirs. We imagined their fury had they tore open the crates hoping to find prized booty and found instead tennis rackets and tuxedos.

But the fate of *Carmen* was sealed. All that day the ship lay helpless on the beach. From deep in the jungle we could hear explosions as Japanese planes pounded her again and again.

On the 27th of December we were quartered

beneath some banana trees in front of a little hut in the jungle. "An odd thing is happening here," I wrote in my diary. "The natives in a barrio have a piano and a little Filipino girl is taking lessons. What a contrast. All the soldiers are standing around watching the lesson. They have a monkey here. The piano teacher is now playing and is she good. Sgt. Sayer played a few songs. We had quite a few air raid alarms but no bombs were dropped here."

I also reported in my diary that my unit had been broken up. Some of the friends I had been with since Letterman were assigned to the 2nd Battalion, others to the 3rd. "I am sitting under a tree with the monkey sleeping in my lap. I have just set up my bed. It is nice and quiet now."

I was assigned as a field medic to Headquarters company, Thirty-first Infantry, the only American infantry regiment in the islands. We took up positions along the front that faced north where the Japanese were certain to come. We knew they were coming.

Chapter 5

THE BASTARDS OF BATAAN

———◆———

Bataan province is in central Luzon of the Philippines, and occupies a 530-square miles (1,370 sq km) peninsula extending southward and sheltering Manila Bay (east) from the South China Sea. Corregidor Island lies just off its southern tip at the entrance of the bay. About 30 miles (48 km) long and averaging 15 miles in width, Bataan is largely covered by jungle and is traversed north to south by steep mountains culminating in Mt. Natib (4,224 ft [1,287 m]) in the north and Mt. Bataan (4,701 ft) in the south...HS

The most effective weapon the Japanese had was their air force. With our fighter planes knocked out and with the little ground fire we had their bombers and fighter planes were over us from morning until dark. The fighters usually flew in flights of three planes. Observation planes working in conjunction with big guns directed artillery fire into our area. We had to keep out of sight at all times.

One morning when we were camped in a gulch, we started to fire our rifles, mostly in frustration, at the planes as they flew over at a low altitude. That afternoon, six planes dove and dropped their bombs on top our line. Causalities were light, but our commanding officer ordered us to stop firing at enemy planes since our fire exposed our position. Blackouts were taken seriously. A man lighting a cigarette after dark, we were told, would be shot.

The little air support we did have included three or four P-40 Warhawks which occasionally flew over our lines. They came from a dirt airstrip at Cabcaban. The strip was maintained for operations and was protected by anti-aircraft guns. There was no doubt, however, that Japanese planes had full control of the entire area.

At the end of each day I looked for a quiet place to write in my diary. Some days there was no such place. Often I wrote when we were under fire. At times like this I felt that if I didn't survive perhaps my diary would, and then the world would know the hell we were going through. But, I had to be careful that I didn't record information that might be harmful to us if the Japanese ever got hold of it. I also knew, military information or not, if I were caught and found with a diary it would mean my instant death.

The following is my account of some of the action that took place during the battle of Abucay. Manila had fallen a few days before on January 2nd, and all the defending American and Filipino forces had withdrawn to Bataan.

This was the Thirty-first Infantry Regiment's first and most important battle. The name Abucay comes from a barrio, or village, located along the eastern coastal plain of the Bataan peninsula. A defensive line was drawn across the peninsula that became known as the Abucay line. American and Filipino troops held this line from January to April of 1942. I like to think it helped to slow down the overall invasion of the South Pacific.

"January 6, 1942: There was much artillery activity during the night. At about 1:00, our 155s were firing very close to us...without any return fire from the Japanese until 10:45. I recognized the first enemy shell whistling towards us and after yelling a warning, we dove into our foxholes. We are directly in the middle of an artillery duel. Our shells as well as enemy shells are whizzing over our heads. Two shells fell closer.

"My foxhole was not deep enough for me so I dashed to another hole and piled in with Sergeant Sayer from my company. Dive bombers have appeared and we are now getting it from the artillery and the bombs. It is a great relief to talk to someone while the shells are exploding. Sergeant Sayer remembered that he had some canned foods in a truck parked nearby. With shells popping around me, I reached the truck and dashed back with the food.

"It is now 7:00 and we haven't had a rest from shell fire all day. We received a call from Major White, our commanding officer, asking for seven men to go to the Third Battalion to aid them with casualties.

"We set off in the dark and, while crossing through our lines, our own men turned a machine gun on us. After much yelling they recognized us and let us pass. We hiked through mud flats and waded across a stream. We weren't sure where the battalion was and also had news that the Japanese had broken through. They were in the vicinity somewhere. We finally found the battalion and discovered that they had not needed us. I was assigned guard duty for two hours and then we received orders to evacuate. We piled in a truck and headed for the mountains, arriving at our destination at 3:00 in the morning, and tried to sleep."

Most of my time from January 7 to January 14 was spent on routine duty. Japanese planes were bombing around our area, but no close hits were registered. They kept us under cover and between bombings and artillery barrages, we kept busy digging first-aid dugouts and foxholes. It was during this time that the phrase "The Bastards of Bataan" originated as we joked about our predicament. No air support, no tanks, very little food, ammunition running low, no Uncle Sam; all this tended to fit the expression, "Bastards of Bataan." The real question that haunted us was were we really bastards of Bataan? Had we been forsaken? The one thing we couldn't give up was hope.

On the 16th, we broke camp and started back toward the front. We hiked about ten miles that night in the dark. All during the march artillery guns were firing around us and we could see a red glow as we approached the front lines. Finally about midnight we left the road and lay down in the brush to sleep. A battery of 155's was nearby and every time the guns fired we were lifted off the ground. We had also been warned to watch for snipers in the area. I did not sleep much that night.

We set up an aid station and from that time until we withdrew on the 24th, we were in the midst of a continuous battle. We received little food and almost no sleep. What follows are my diary entries for the 23rd and 24th.

"January 23, 1942: Our artillery opened up before daylight on an advance. Noise was terrific. Guns are within a few hundred yards of us. I was awakened and put on guard duty until breakfast time. After breakfast I went back to bed. At daybreak Jap bombers dropped bombs at our artillery. They were quite close. A battery of long distance Jap guns started to shell our area at 8:00 in the morning. Shells are whizzing overhead.

"At 11:30, our guns started firing back at them. The noise is deafening. Planes are bombing around our artillery positions. It is getting hotter every minute! Japanese artillery has scored a direct hit on something. We can hear flames crackling.

"12:55: we are lucky to be alive. Three Jap bombers have just dropped a load of bombs on us. The concussion shook us up and we were covered with dirt and branches from the trees that were over us. It felt like somebody slapped me in the mouth. We administered first-aid to several men and had to treat severely shell-shocked soldiers. The trees we were under were torn to shreds.

"Shells are still exploding around us and planes are

overhead. We were called to help an artillery unit and found two men dead and several wounded. After taking care of casualties, we walked back to camp with planes overhead. We were under shell fire continuously. We had to hit the dirt many times.

"January 24, 1942: 11:30: Japanese are opening up with artillery fire this morning. Shells are exploding right in camp. They are bursting within ten to three hundred yards. Four of us are piled in a large foxhole. We were covered with dirt and shrapnel was buzzing all around us. Only three casualties.

"5:00: Sent out detail to recover two wounded men. As soon as we started up the road, shells commenced to drop around us. We found out that the wounded men had already been carried out. After coming back to camp, I decided to take a bath. I stripped and started to wash in an irrigation ditch. No sooner was the soap applied than the shells started to come over. I was trapped in the nude and had to drop into the shallow ditch until the shelling ceased.

"We received word that Goukus, a medical man and a good friend, had been picked off by a sniper.

"At 8 o'clock the whole 31st started to withdraw. We fell into single file formation without anything to eat and marched towards the Mariveles Mountains. We marched until 1:30 am and then had our chow and laid on the ground to sleep. We were dog tired. One man passed out on the road."

Chapter 6

AT HOME IN THE JUNGLE

———◆◆———

Every soldier trapped in a foxhole during an artillery barrage faces a stiff test of self-control. Many times I struggled through this ordeal and forced myself to relax when I felt like screaming, jumping out of my foxhole, and dashing madly through the jungle. There were occasions, while the shells were bursting around me, when my thoughts wandered back to some incident during my boyhood days. It were these thoughts that kept me from going mad.

On this morning I remembered my first experience with death. I was three years old. It is early morning and I am standing in the kitchen clutching my mama's hand, certain that the trap door of my underwear is open in back. A burly policeman stands in the room. He holds a pad and a pencil in his hands and he is trying to get information from my mother but there is a problem: His questions are coming out in a heavy Irish brogue and my mama is responding in wild and gesticulating Italian. Tony, my older brother—he is six—is trying unsuccessfully to translate.

A band of thieves had raided our block that night during a rainstorm. Several basements were rifled. At approximately the same time that the hoodlums were engaged in the looting, a patrolman had come around the corner, innocently walking his beat. As he started up the street, a volley of loud shots shattered the stillness of the night and running footsteps echoed through the deep cellars. A light suddenly went on in an upper flat next door, and in quick succession three shots rang out and bullets pierced the illuminated windows. Broken glass shattered to the pavement below and immediately the light was extinguished. A deep ominous silence settled over the neighborhood.

Papa showed more intelligence. He jumped out of bed, drew the curtain slowly aside, and peeked through the window. Directly below him, two men were sneaking through the fence. Papa promptly pulled the curtain tight and hopped back in bed.

The following morning, after many futile attempts to obtain some sort of intelligible statement from Mama, the policeman slowly climbed the stairs to the next floor, muttering and shaking his head. We tried to tell him that Aunt Mary lived upstairs and that she couldn't speak English either, but he didn't understand.

My brother Tony went down to the corner and saw the dead patrolman. He was lying on the wet pavement and his feet were pointed toward the door of the saloon. I remembered Tony's description of the dead man as I lay in the foxhole.

The Thirty-first Infantry repulsed the Japanese and held its position, at least for the present. We were replaced by Philippine army units and we moved to a bivouac area behind the lines. Instead of a welcoming respite from battle, it proved to be unpleasant, hiding from the enemy and waiting for something to happen.

The bivouac area was located in a heavily wooded area well screened from enemy planes. A beautiful mountain stream flowed through mango and bamboo groves. It was beautiful but deadly! The water was cool and crystal clear, and it looked much like the mountain streams back home in northern California. But it was not like the streams at home. In the mountain steams of Bataan dwelled those tiny microbes that bring on dysentery. And dysentery in the tropics, more often than not, can be fatal.

We were ordered not to touch a drop of water unless it was treated. I was put in charge of chlorinating the drinking water that we kept in a large canvas bag hanging from a tree. Every day we changed the water and added chlorine to make it safe to drink, but unfortunately the chlorine wasn't always effective.

Enemy planes constantly flew above our jungle hideout but the foliage was so dense we were able to move around without danger of being sighted from the air.

When we first arrived, I had looked around for a safe place to sleep. I chose an irrigation ditch nearby that was about six feet wide. With a machete a Filipino had given me I cut down a couple dozen bamboo poles and placed them across the ditch. I then laid layers of grass over the poles and thus made myself a comfortable accommodation. I slept well the first two nights but on the third morning my bones were aching. I blamed the discomfort on my bed and did some rearranging. On the fourth morning I awoke so stiff I found it difficult to walk. Every bone in my body ached horribly and I had a high temperature. I knew the symptoms. I feared I might have a case of dysentery coming on. I reported to the camp doctor and was informed that I had contacted dengue fever, a disease found in the tropics commonly known as "breakbone fever." Much like malaria, it's carried by mosquitos, but it's not always fatal. Fortunately, the doctor still had medicine which he gave me and in a few days I felt much better.

More than the Japanese, our worst enemy during this period was the anopheles mosquito. Our scenic bivouac area was infested by this mosquito. Though this malaria-carrying insect generally conducts his deadly air raids at night, they may chose to attack during the day as well as night. Without nets we were helpless. We were constantly bitten, from head to toe, and the effects of their bites soon began to take its toll. At first, only a few men were sent back to the hospital area located about twenty kilometers behind the lines. Before long the numbers increased until they reached alarming proportions. Something had to be done and quickly.

Our commanding officer sent a detail to search for another area. I was ordered to go with this group and, after hiking through the jungle, we found a spot similar to the one we were leaving. It too had a mountain stream but seemingly with less mosquitos. I chose my own bedding down area and we then returned and made our report to the C.O. He agreed fully to the change of scene.

To my delight, I found several banana groves in the new area. I devised a method to get the bananas down without chopping down the trees, trees which helped serve as cover. I tied my machete to a long bamboo pole and cut down the bunches of bananas by hacking through the stems, leaving the groves still standing. The bananas were still green so I dug a couple of holes and carefully buried them. I had learned from the Filipinos that this method speeded up their ripening. I felt proud of myself that I was learning a few things about life in the jungle.

Over next few days we moved our outfit and settled into the new area. Then I surprised my friends by digging up the bananas. They had fully ripened. We quickly and ravenously feasted on them with little ceremony. After that I kept a stash of bananas buried in the ground and used them to trade for other items of food. Everyone called me the "King of the Bananas," and over the next few weeks I ate so many bananas that I became tired of them in spite of still being hungry. I ate banana sandwiches, bananas with rice, bananas with condensed milk. I ate bananas with whatever I could find.

A man I knew found a radio which we hooked up to a truck battery. In the evening, with the sounds of insects buzzing all around us and unknown animals calling out in the jungle, we would listen to a news program from home called "The Voice of Freedom." As news spread about that we had a radio, the crowd at evening news time grew larger and larger and often included high ranking officers. After the news the station played American music, mostly big band music that was so popular at that time. Like the hymns the nurses had sung before Christmas, the music brought with it powerful images of home. I literally felt like crying when I listened to it every night, as probably did every other soldier gathered around that truck. Still, there was something soothing and fine about the music, and when conditions permitted I enjoyed going to sleep listening to it. Sometimes during the day we tuned in to Tokyo and could listen to the Japanese propaganda broadcasts. According to the Japanese, we had been completely wiped out, totally eliminated.

Our company's move into this new area did not solve the malaria problem as we had thought it might. The anopheles mosquitoes simply followed us to our new site, and now they struck with savage vengeance. More and more men became stricken with the fever and had to be sent back to the base hospital. We felt there would soon be no one left to defend our lines.

For about two months now we had now been under constant Japanese air attacks and unrelenting shelling. Food had became scarce. We had nearly exhausted our rations, and we were not being resupplied. We turned to eating dead horses and mules that had been killed from the blasts of bombs and shells. We were given something to eat in the morning, and then something in the evening. If we wanted something to eat during the day, we had to do our own improvising. One day the mess sergeant came up with canned abalone. Lord knows where he found it but he did. I remembered the abalone sandwiches my friends and I had enjoyed just before we left San Francisco and I was excited at the prospect of having some now. Our excitement soon turned to bitter disappointment. The abalone was tougher than shoe leather. Hides from the dead horses and mules would have served better.

Our search for food took us into the jungle. We had heard that Filipinos ate monkeys, and, in fact, considered them a delicacy. A friend and I decided to hunt for monkeys. After hiking through the dense forest for a few hours, we suddenly heard a loud squawking noise. We found a wild chicken hopping up and down in the bushes. We moved in only to find it was tied to a string. I was just about to grab it when a Filipino appeared from nowhere and claimed it.

The Filipino demonstrated his trap for us. It was ingenious to say the least. Bamboo slats about two feet long were placed in the ground a couple of inches apart to form a fence about fifty feet long. An opening was left in the middle for the chicken to squeeze through. At the opening, a string was attached to a small tree with a trigger made from twigs. The tree was bent over to form a spring and the string made into a loop with a slip knot. The whole concept of this trap depended on the chicken's low I.Q. A hen or rooster would never jump or fly over the fence. It always preferred to follow the fence until it came to an opening, so the Filipino explained.

The next day my friend and I hiked backed into the hills and set a trap as the Filipino had taught us. The following morning we rushed to the snare to see if we had caught anything. Much to our dismay we found nothing, but we did see feathers scattered around the area. We had caught a chicken, that was certain, but someone had gotten to it before we did.

These experiences made me feel more confident in the jungle and some nights when I wanted to be alone,

I left my foxhole and slept by myself in the brush. I did this a number of times, until one night I heard rustling in the bush all around me. I thought I might be surrounded by Japanese soldiers. I crawled on hands and knees back to my foxhole and never again slept alone in the jungle.

During this period we moved around periodically, always setting up a new aid station wherever we settled. Many men, myself included, suffered from diarrhea and fever. Our travels generally took us deeper into the Mariveles Mountains. Japanese planes continued to circle over us and frequently bombed facilities close at hand. On February 7th I reported in my diary: "This spot is the most beautiful we have been to. We are in the primeval jungle. We have a mountain stream and the thick foliage makes it quite cool all day long. We are located behind our artillery and all we have to worry about is anti-aircraft shrapnel."

At each stop we had to make new sleeping arrangements. On the 10th of February I made the following entry: "At 3:00 in the morning Marchesi's bed broke and he fell to the ground. I thought it was funny. An hour later my bed broke and I fell five feet. I slept on the ground for the rest of the night."

On the 16th, Hendrickson and I hitched a ride to Hospital No. 2 to visit old friends and see if I could find out what had happened to my accordion. Someone must have seen it. We ran into quite a lot of guys from Letterman. One of them told me he had found the accordion and left it with a woman in Manila.

I visited the hospital cemetery and saw rows of graves marked with little bamboo crosses. Our friends at the hospital treated us to special dish—caramel pudding, made from canned sweetened condensed milk that had been boiled for an hour, then allowed to cool. This they mixed with canned fruit. No dish has ever tasted better.

On a couple of occasions I traveled as far as Hospital No. 1, a distance of more the 20 kilometers. Several of my Letterman friends were there, and they had a much better supply of food. While I was touring the hospital I met Miss Kuethahl, the nurse who had been my instructor at Sternberg. She asked me if I would like to transfer to the hospital, saying she needed me. I told her I would think about it. After giving it serious thought, a few days later I went to see her and said I would like to transfer. It was too late. Before the paperwork could be accomplished things changed suddenly.

Chapter 7

THE LAST STAND

Lt. John Bulkerley, commander of PT-41, received orders to proceed to Corregidor. The high command had to be evacuated, by orders of the President of the United States. On March 11, 1942, General Douglas MacArthur, his wife and their son were taken aboard PT-41, and they made rendezvous with three other boats from the Squadron Six at the entrance to Manila Bay and together proceeded south. It was not an easy voyage.

A strong easterly wind made the going rough, with sheets of water crashing over the bows. Before the night was over the boats became separated. Passengers and crew alike aboard PT-41 were drenched and exhausted when they reached their destination, but they had made the trip of 912 kms through Japanese-patrolled waters and had arrived precisely on time. Later that day the other boats reached port.

Lt. Bulkerley returned with PT-41 to the fighting in the north. They fought until there were no more torpedoes available. In the end, PT-41 was set afire by its own crew to keep it from falling in the hands of the Japanese...HS

News reached us that General Douglas MacArthur, our commander-in-chief, had left Corregidor. We heard through the grapevine that he had boarded a torpedo boat and was ordered to Australia. We were told we now had a new commander, General Jonathan Wainwright.

The news that MacArthur had left caused great concern among the troops. Rumors and speculation ran wild. Some believed "Dugout Doug," as they called him, had deserted us. I didn't feel this way at all. I reasoned he was following orders and had no other choice. The President of the United States ordered him to leave and to reorganize so that our troops could return. My concern now was not so much as how long could we hold out but how long would the war last. We were also concerned with our more immediate problems, like the coming rains.

Rumors began circulating around camp that we would probably spend the rainy season, usually a long six months, in the jungle. Having little to do other than wait for the Japanese to come, I decided to build myself a small hut and prepare for the rains. A few G.I.s thought I was crazy. Why put myself thorough all that work, they said, and I might not be around long enough to use the hut? What did it matter? I knew well it was much better to keep busy than be idle.

With my trusty machete as my only tool, I cut down large bamboo poles about six feet long and eight inches in diameter. These I notched for the foundation. I dug holes and placed the notched poles into the ground, and then laced crosspieces into the notches. To make a floor, I split several bamboo poles into narrow slats and strung these to the crosspieces. Next came the bamboo uprights. These I tied up to the foundation with strips of bamboo I had soaked in water to make pliable. The roof I made from grass that I had stripped and salvaged from the roof of an abandoned shack.

My trim little hut made me very proud, and it appeared that I would be quite comfortable when the rains came. I moved in when the roof was completed.

In the evening of April 2nd, Lieutenant Brown, Sergeant Sayer and I climbed to the crest of a hill to watch the moon rise. We could see the bay and Manila in the distance. The moonlight filtering through a few scattered clouds was beautiful. As I sat and gazed out at the lovely scene, I became very homesick. I wanted to cry right there. It was sad to know how helpless we were to do anything. Why did we have to die?

I envisioned my home, my sister and brothers, and my friends. I dreamed of the day I would step into my home once more. As we sat there on the crest of the hill, thinking and dreaming about home, we had no way of knowing we would be spending our last night in the jungle camp, or that one week later we would be prisoners of the Japanese. This was our last taste of freedom for the years to come.

At dusk the next day we were called together and told to prepare ourselves to move into action. A big battle was coming. Our most senior officer addressed us in a solemn voice. He assured us we would have support in our endeavor to hold the line. Tanks would be in front of us, he said, and P-40's overhead to protect us. At nine o'clock with moonlight streaming through the trees we broke camp and again started toward the front lines. For a brief while the truck I was in got lost from the rest of the convoy. We finally found our outfit at midnight. We pulled off the road, stretched our blankets on the ground and went to sleep.

The next morning, as we were digging in, wave after wave of Japanese bombers came in from the north and dropped their bombs all around us. There were no tanks to be seen, nor P-40s overhead as promised. After chow we were again ordered to leave our foxholes and move toward the front.

Just as we were about a hundred yards from camp, I remembered my canteen. I had forgotten it and ran back to get it. Suddenly, halfway there, I stopped dead in my tracks. The path was blocked! Standing directly in front of me, with tongue licking out and tail lashing back and forth, was what I thought at first to be a prehistoric dragon, a living dinosaur. I then realized I was face to face with a Komoto lizard. He was at least six feet long, and had he wished, he could have had me for lunch. How would my family react to this news: Son killed in battle, eaten by a dragon? I didn't give the animal the slightest chance to act. In no time at all I was back to the truck, without my canteen.

I was detailed to drive the truck. We left at dusk and I had a difficult time finding the road in the dark. A soldier named Jackson sat on the front fender and helped to guide me over the narrow, difficult dirt road. We were moving toward Mt. Samat, the scene of our final battle. As we drove, artillery shells burst around us on every flank.

A T-shirted Japanese colonel arranges Bataan's surrender with Major General King (left).

Chapter 8

THE FALL OF BATAAN

———◆———

During the final days of the battle for Bataan, American and
Filipino forces attempted to form a line of resistance across the
peninsula from Orion on Manila Bay to Bagac on the South
China Sea. At the mountainous center of this line was Mt. Samat,
a 2,000 foot, conical peak. On April 5, 1942, the Japanese 4th
Division under General Taniguchi and the 61st Infantry regiment
under Colonel Sato moved against the mountain from the north
and fought their way to the summit. The high ground secured,
the Japanese moved rapidly down Samat's southern slope,
penetrating Bataan's last line of defense...HS

My account of the fighting that lasted for four days
on the slopes of Mount Samat is relived in the following
entries in my diary. It appears exactly as I wrote it.

"April 6, 1942: Up at daybreak. We were greeted with
rifle and machine gun fire and strafing by enemy planes.
Three of us dug a foxhole immediately. While digging
the hole, we had to fall flat on our faces many times
because of mortar, machine gun, and rifle fire. We ate
our canned rations for breakfast. They had just come from
Corregidor. After we ate, dive bombers dove over us and
bombed close by. Observation planes are continually flying
overhead.

"At 10:00, the enemy artillery commenced to shell
our positions. The fire was heavy and shells were passing
overhead. Japanese opened up with machine gun and rifle
fire again. One of our sergeants dashed from the
command post and yelled to us that we have five minutes
to load the truck and to retreat for our lives. It was reported
that Philippine army units were supposed to withdraw

slowly and we were to counterattack. Our patrols this morning found that the Philippine army was forced to withdrew during the night and we were now stranded.

"I drove the truck as fast as I could and we put up an aid station in the bed of a creek. Dive bombers were over us all of the time and we couldn't move in our tracks. We were resting in the afternoon for a few moments when we received news that the enemy was again coming down the road in great numbers. We were again given orders to get out quickly. As we left we could hear rifle and machine gun fire coming toward us. I again drove the truck down the road, which was littered with all sort of troops. We pulled up at our old camp and dive bombers commenced to strafe and bomb us. We remained in our holes for about one hour while we were being strafed by enemy planes. We received news that the First and Second Battalions were fighting for their lives in their withdrawal.

"I am exhausted. I haven't had any sleep for twenty-four hours. This is getting rugged. We ate our canned rations and I was detailed to act as stand-by runner for the night for Captain Rader, our new commanding officer.

"April 7 , 1942: Up at daybreak. We were given orders to load the truck and to be ready once more. Four men, including myself, went back up to the First Battalion and I was left as a guard for one hour. While watching the truck, low-flying planes kept circling and banking over me. I had to keep retreating Filipinos away. After being relieved from duty, I had a can of rations and cold coffee. Planes were overhead all the time. Just as I lay down to rest, one of the men shouted for us to get out immediately. We all hopped on the truck, and when we pulled away snipers opened up on us. We recognized Captain Brennan, a medical officer in command of the Third Battalion medics, in a dazed condition, being helped down the road. We stopped and piled him into the truck. The dust was terrific. An old bus stalled in front of me and I had to push it out of the way. One of our men finally stopped us and I drove the truck under a bamboo thicket. Bombs were dropping around us. Enemy shells were whizzing overhead.

"I am sitting in a foxhole resting. It is 10:25 in the morning. At 10:30, we again started back in a rush. Planes over us all the time. We went over to our last camp and are now awaiting further orders. I lay in a foxhole and tried to get some rest while dive bombers and artillery fire were going full blast. An American patrol came in and told us the Japanese were right on our tail. There was a mad dash for trucks and cars. Again, I hopped into my truck and all the boys jumped in with me. We drove through a shell-torn area with trucks and cars littering the road. In many places, we had to detour around bomb craters.

"By the grace of God, the sky seemed to be clear of planes for about one-half an hour. Troops were all over the road. We finally arrived at the main road and I really tore along. Bombers were overhead, but we did not stop for them. We drove back to one of our old bivouac areas and got out and took a bath and washed all the dust from our bodies. I found an automobile with the clutch gone and managed to get it started. We left for the Second Corps area to get information. On the way, we ran into our company and commanding officer, Captain Rader. We were certainly glad to see him. I received instructions to take the truck and men back to a service company for chow. Returning to the truck, we found one of our boys who was shell shocked and rambling aimlessly down the road. I picked him up and left him with an ambulance. We then started off and arrived at the service company at 6:00. We had our chow and then the bombers started again and kept us flat on our faces for about one hour. They were diving and bombing all around us. They finally left and we drove back to our camp. Sergeant Sayer and I spent the night in the hut I had built and I slept very well as I was exhausted.

"April 8, 1942: Up at 4:00. We moved our vehicles out, ready to evacuate. Foot troops walked past us. Our commanding officer left and we ate some canned rations. We put the vehicles back under cover and sat near our holes. We set up an aid station and worked on men all day. The men that are coming in are exhausted, blistered, shaken up, discouraged, and covered with dirt and grime. The tales they tell us are unbelievable. They have been wandering aimlessly through the jungle, searching for their companies and officers. Many of them have been bombed and are stunned, some of them in tears. They all are still hoping for help even though it looks like a suicide regiment.

"Planes have been bombing over us all day, big bombers and dive bombers. At 6:00, we were suddenly told that the enemy was just about at our road intersection. I drove the truck out of the brush and everybody hopped on. Planes were overhead. We dashed for the intersection, which was about three kilometers ahead, and we took an alternate road and crossed a creek. Two tanks and half-tracks were covering the retreat. Troops were cluttering the road. Machine gun and rifle fire was very close. I drove the truck down the road and there were all kinds of vehicles on the edge of the road. We slowed down as it became dark and finally turned into a motor-pool area at Kilometer Post 167. We took blankets, walked to a camp, lay on the ground and went to sleep.

"April 9, 1942: During the night, we had a strong earthquake. It woke us all up. An hour later, we were all awakened again by ammunition dumps exploding. We had to move down into a gully. We arose at 6:00 and then gathered with about a hundred other soldiers. Word is going around that we have surrendered. It is now 7:00. I am looking around at these men. It is pitiful. They are stunned and disheartened. Fighting is still going on all around us. We took cover in some dugouts. Sergeant Sayer went out to try and find someone who knows something. As I lay in this foxhole I still have hope and faith in Uncle Sam. He will not desert us in this hour of need. We have been without nourishing food for two months. We have been suffering from malaria and dysentery. The men should never have been sent up to the front this last time. They were much too weak. They were being bombed, strafed and torn to shreds. I believe that the Thirty-first Infantry is no more. All that was needed was a few planes. I have failed to write about the men's condition, because I did not want to divulge any military information. But now I am writing this, because I know it won't make any difference. I went to a mess kitchen and had to wait an hour for some rice. Bombers are over us continually. After eating I laid down to sleep. I was awakened by someone shouting...."

That incomplete sentence terminates my diary. There was no more time to write. I shoved the book into my pocket and forgot about it for the time being.

Bataan falls into Japanese hands.

Chapter 9

THE SURRENDER

——◆——

The Bataan Death March was a forced march of more than 70,000 American and Filipino prisoners of war captured by the Japanese in the Philippines in the early stages of World War II. Starting out on April 9, 1942, from Manveles on the southern end of the Bataan Peninsula, they were force-marched 55 miles to San Fernando, where some were taken by rail to Capas, and from here they all walked the final eight miles to Camp O'Donnell. They were starved and mistreated, often kicked or beaten on the way, and many who fell and couldn't continue were bayonetted where they lay. Their bodies were left to rot in the sun. Only 54,000 reached the camp; some 7 000-10,000 died on the way and the rest escaped to the jungle...HS

On that morning of April 9, 1942, our officers told us to stack our arms. They announced the fearful news that our American and Filipino forces on Bataan had surrendered. They further ordered us to march out to the main road that extended from Mariveles to San Fernando. As it so sadly turned out, this was the start of the infamous Bataan Death March.

At the intersection we encountered our first live Japanese soldier. He was an officer, standing alone, and he treated us courteously. He motioned for us to march farther down the main road, which we did. After about a hundred yards we stopped and lined up on both sides of the road and waited. We waited for the victorious Japanese army on its way to take up positions opposite Corregidor. Soon came tanks, artillery pieces, and finally foot soldiers by the hundreds.

A close friend, Charlie Wright, stood next to me.

"Don't worry. They're not going to hurt us," he said. He was smiling. A Japanese solder saw him smiling, rushed up and slapped him hard across the face. He then grabbed Charlie's arm and yanked away his wrist watch. Charlie stood there in awe, the smile gone from his face.

Word now spread through our ranks, "get rid of your Jap stuff." I didn't know what "Jap stuff" they were talking about but I would find out.

Soon Japanese soldiers, noncommissioned officers and three-star privates, broke ranks, rushed up and struck our men for no reason. They hit them with open hands, fists and rifle butts. They began searching our persons, and then went through our packs, confiscating what they wanted. They took our watches, rings, fountain pens, whatever valuables they found. Some even took our shoes. Their officers did nothing to stop them, and, in fact, only seemed to encourage them on, like one does to a dog to force him to attack.

When the soldiers found anything stamped with Japanese markings they went into an uncontrollable rage. An U.S. soldier possessing a shaving mirror with "Made In Japan" markings was beaten unmercifully. Another with Japanese souvenir money was kicked until he became unconscious. The Japanese obviously thought we had taken these items from their dead. We lost no time discarding anything that was Japanese or even resembled Japanese.

After the vanguard of soldiers had passed, armed guards with fixed bayonets herded us into an open field. We had nothing to eat that day, nor any water to drink. We slept on the hard ground without blankets or nets. Mosquitos attacked us with the same determination as dive bombers had the day before.

The next morning our guards ordered us to our feet and herded us back onto the road. We were told to march up the road toward San Fernando, a railroad junction about fifty-five miles distant. We had walked only a short distance when more Japanese soldiers heading to the front came down the road. They too broke ranks, searched and beat us at will. Some became highly angered when they could find nothing of value in our possession. Thereafter we were stopped often to allow more Japanese soldiers and equipment to pass. Their ferocity grew as we marched on into the afternoon. Our stragglers, the men too weak to keep up, were the worst victims. The Japanese were no longer content to maul those who fell behind, or prick them with bayonet points; their thrusts now were meant to kill. The fate of those who fell behind we didn't know. We never saw them again.

Mile after mile the looting and beatings continued. They cared not whom they struck. High ranking officers were no exception. I watched one three-star private attack Major General Edward King, the U.S. commander who surrendered our troops on Bataan. Had we been sitting in movie theater, we might have thought we were watching a Charley Chaplin comedy, but in reality there was nothing funny about it. The soldier was so short that he had to jump to strike the general in the face with his fist. He did it time and time again, and the general just stood there. I was only a few yards away and I could do nothing. No one could do anything. Guards with pointed rifles waited for us to do something. Finally, the private gave up in disgust and walked away.

No food was given to us that day either. Again we camped in an open field upon hard ground. We had covered but five miles that day on our way to San Fernando. At the rate we were going, it would take us another ten days, and by then most of us would be dead.

As we were bedding down I noticed a wide shallow stream next to our camp site. Before attempting to sleep

I decided to clean up. Without guards noticing I made my way to the stream, undressed and lay down in the water. I heard noises up stream. I focused my attention and discovered the sounds were coming from a group of Japanese soldiers who were spreading a fish net across the stream. I kept low and watched. A small fish, much like a perch, had been stunned by the net and it floated down stream toward me. I grabbed it, shut my eyes, and gulped it down. Another came by and then several more. I ravenously swallowed them whole, wiggling and alive.

Early the next morning, impatient Japanese soldiers stepped among us and kicked us awake. We were just as exhausted now as we had been when we went to sleep. We were each given a small ball of rice and once again we began ambling down the road more toward San Fernando. The sun burned away the morning dew, and before long the hot surface of the road blistered our feet. The temperature rose by the minute. Noon came and went. The midday heat was scorching and unrelenting. We craved water, even the mud-filth water that lay in the sinkholes in the fields would have sufficed but we could not break ranks. If we had, even to drink the filthy water, death would have followed.

Rumors were now spreading that we were going directly to Manila instead of San Fernando. We also heard that the Japanese needed drivers for the abandoned American trucks scattered along the route. Thinking that I might drive prisoners to Manila, I volunteered. After explaining that I had been a truck driver in America, which I had been, I was selected along with several other prisoners.

A Japanese officer escorted us several miles back over the road from which we had come, and almost immediately I began to wonder if I had done the right thing. I began cursing to myself that I had volunteered, and realized that I had no idea what I was getting into. Maybe it was another of their sadistic games created for their own sordid self amusement.

I was relieved to learn the mission was legitimate and not a prank. The officer led us to a six-wheel GMC truck with three axles; it was resting helplessly in a ditch beside the road. It appeared at a glance to be in fair condition. As I got into the cab to drive, a Japanese soldier with the rank of private superior climbed in with me, to act as my guard. He had extremely short legs and a mouth filled with gold teeth. He was as sinister looking as any enemy soldier I had so far seen. His actions and his general behavior immediately made me suspicious of his mental stability. Nevertheless, I was aware I had to humor him in any way I could.

The engine turned over, sending out puffs of smoke, and after a couple jerky starts, more for display on my part, we were on our way. The soldier sitting next to me smiled with approval.

The fury of the recent battle was in evidence everywhere one turned. Trees had been stripped from the bomb blasts; the earth marred with shell crater after shell crater and pieces of wrecked equipment were strewn over the road. Japanese infantry soldiers continued streaming south toward the beach that faced Corregidor. We were forced to pull over and stop many times due to heavy traffic snarls. The dust became choking. At all times, on both sides of the truck, I was surrounded by enemy soldiers. Some eyed me curiously, not knowing what to make of my presence; others looked as though they would have liked very much to get their hands on me. An engine failure would probably have meant my life. I prayed it didn't happen. As long as we kept moving, or the engine was running, I felt relatively safe behind the wheel.

My demented private superior guard didn't make

*Prisoners, their hands tied behind their backs and gaunt from
starvation and lack of water, get a moment's respite. Beatings
of slow or recalcitrant continued during these intervals.*

matters any better. He couldn't sit there contented to let me drive. He continuously tried to impress his fellow soldiers with his knowledge of American trucks. Every time we stopped in traffic, he would get out of the cab, lift the hood, and start tinkering with the wires. Several times he crawled under the truck to pretend he was making an adjustment of some sort. I held my breath at his antics, afraid of what damage he might do.

As we drove along, bodies of the dead littered both sides of the road. The smell of decaying flesh, swarming with flies, was nauseating. I came around one rather sharp curve and saw, to my horror, two dead American soldiers in the path of the truck. There was nothing I could do, surrounded as I was by Japanese soldiers. I had to drive over their bodies. It wasn't long after that incident that the one thing I feared most did happen. The truck's engine faltered and we stopped dead in our tracks.

I quickly forgot the two dead soldiers I had crushed beneath my wheels and leaped out of the cab. Before my feet touched the ground I was surrounded a group of enemy soldiers. One grinning soldier, in a display of superiority among his peers, began beating me about the head and shoulder with a large heavy flashlight. Blood ran down my forehead and neck. I was sure my end was near, but just then another soldier ran up and began jabbering in Japanese. The soldier with the flashlight stopped beating me. The second soldier was pointing to the medical corps red cross on my shirt.

"Doctor, doctor," he said in heavily accented English, and soon several other men repeated the word. They ·backed away and let me get back in the truck. My life was spared again.

Meanwhile, my guard who couldn't have cared less about my safety, continued to tinker with the truck. He opened the hood, pulled at some wires, and crawled under the truck several times. I was worried that he would do more damage than good so I got back out of the cab to check the electrical system. I found that the battery ground cable was nearly rotted out. I was relieved to find an old school bus nearby with a useable cable still in place. I removed the cable from the bus and transferred it to the truck. I climbed into the cab, stepped on the starter and the engine started to purr. The guard flashed his gold teeth.

After travelling a few hours, we pulled off the road for some much needed sleep. I chose a spot in the back of the truck where I couldn't easily be spotted. Lying there, I thought seriously about trying to escape to the hills and maybe meet up with the resistance force, if there were one. Soldiers in the first few days did escape but we never knew if they made it or not. I finally decided against it, as the area was teeming with Japanese soldiers, some of them leading dogs on leashes. Another deciding factor was that I lacked medicine of any kind to protect me from dysentery or malaria. I decided I would stay with the truck for the time being.

We continued with our motor trip the next morning. We had traveled only a short distance when the guard motioned for me to stop. There was nothing in the road, and no one was around. What did he want now? He shoved me aside with the point of his rifle and then got behind the wheel. He motioned for me to be seated next to him on the front seat. The poor fellow, his legs were so short he had difficulty reaching the clutch and brake pedal. But he was determined he was going to drive the vehicle. This nearly proved fatal.

It happened when we rounded a sharp curve and he suddenly panicked and froze at the wheel. The vehicle ran off the road and came to rest at a very sharp angle, almost tipping over. He motioned for me to wait while he went to get help, and as I watched him disappear down the road I feared he might not come back. As much as I detested him, he was my security. A half hour later he did return, sitting next to the driver in an U.S. military truck, with a second truck following close behind. Both trucks had Japanese drivers.

With the help of winches, we were able to pull our truck back onto the road. I surmised that we must be near our destination, since my guard continued to drive. It was obvious he didn't want to lose face with the other drivers. He most likely told them it was I who drove off the road.

By late afternoon we arrived at an artillery camp. When they saw us, Japanese soldiers came running to greet us and soon flooded around, cheering and throwing up their arms in jubilation. My guard was a hero. I'm sure he made them believe he had driven all the way from the main road to camp. A soldier offered me his canteen but I hesitated. He saw my reluctance and insisted I take a swallow. I did, slowly, and was surprised at the sweetness of the drink. It was sugared tea. It greatly refreshed me. I r ever knew a drink could be so enjoyable.

I was allowed to walk around the camp, but to my disgust, I found I was unable to avoid stepping on human excreta. It was obvious the Japanese were also suffering from dysentery. But there was a difference between American and Japanese soldiers. In American camps our first chore, no matter where we were, was to dig a hole for human waste. Apparently the Japanese didn't take time or didn't care about sanitation. It didn't seem to matter where they relieved themselves. I didn't do much walking about the area that day.

The next morning I discovered the reason why the truck I had been driving was so badly needed. A dozen or more grunting soldiers, sweating profusely, dragged a heavy Japanese artillery piece mounted on wagon wheels from under cover which they hastily attached it to the rear of the truck. It was First World War vintage. No sooner was it in place when a non-commissioned officer motioned for me to get behind the wheel. My guard once again climbed in beside me, somewhat chagrined that he wasn't driving.

A short distance up the road two Japanese trucks were attempting to climb a small hill but were having difficulty in spite of a platoon of soldiers pushing for all their worth. This was my chance to show them American ingenuity. I put my GMC six-wheeler in low gear, and still towing the artillery piece, roared up the hill easily. Once we reached the top I feared that I might have made a grave mistake but the soldiers voiced their approval with shouts and waving arms. We made the rest of the trip to the main road without a problem.

At the intersection, my guard, who was now quite annoyed, motioned for me to get in the back. He climbed into the cab and after grinding gears and a couple rough bumps he somehow managed to get us rolling. The road was heavy with traffic. The Japanese were moving their big guns and ammunition in what seemed like a race to reach the Bataan shore to strengthen their positions opposite Corregidor. Traffic became snarled every few hundred yards. Each time we halted on an incline it would take a few seconds for my guard to apply his short legs to the brakes. During the interval, the truck would roll backwards, causing the gun we were towing to turn in the opposite direction. After several close calls, the truck finally rolled back too far, tipping the artillery piece over in the middle of the road. There was a much yelling and screaming around the accident. I ducked lower in the back of the truck. I didn't dare watch the proceedings for fear they might decide it was my fault. After a half hour of grueling pushing and pulling, the gun was righted and we continued on toward our destination. The officer in charge gave me some rice and a small can of pineapple.

The next morning my guard got behind the wheel before anyone could say anything and then motioned for me to sit on the passenger side. Six officers climbed in back of the truck and we started southward down the main road. Along the way, slowly and painfully marching northward in columns of four, we saw groups of American soldiers being prodded by Japanese guards. They were a pitiful sight, gaunt and hollowed-eyed, hardly able to place one foot in front of the other.

We delivered the officers to a camp a few miles down the road and just as we started back, several artillery shells burst quite close to us. Our forces on Corregidor were returning fire. During the night I had heard several shells coming in from the island. We were still holding out on Corregidor!

Another shell exploded extremely close, forcing us to come to a halt. Through our shattered windshield I saw an American soldier, still alive, lying upon the ground. He had been apparently wounded from the last shell fire. A second shell came our way, exploded a few yards away and covered us with dust and flying debris.

This was my chance to do something. I was becoming more and more disturbed about the antics of my guard and worried about what he might do given the right chance. I now saw my opportunity to escape. I pointed to the wounded soldier and jumped down from the truck. The guard screamed and gesticulated for me to get back in the truck. He apparently figured he might still need me and I'm sure for that reason he didn't shoot me on the spot. Or maybe he was just too preoccupied with the gears to think of anything else. Whatever, I ignored him.

At that moment another shell exploded nearby,

again scattering debris all around us. The guard completely forgot me. He decided to get out of the area as fast as he could. He gunned the motor and with gears grinding and wheels spinning he left me standing in the road.

I discovered another wounded soldier a short distance away. This man, as well as the one I had seen from the window of the truck, had been hit in the leg, but neither seemed to be in very bad shape. Both were officers, a lieutenant and a colonel.

Fearful of more artillery shells, I decided to get these two wounded men out of the area in any way I could. Truck loads of Japanese soldiers streamed by in both directions. I attempted to flag them down but they would not stop. However, they kept pointing to the rear. I sat at the side of the road holding the two wounded officers, and in a few minutes an American truck with a G.I. driver came down the road. He stopped and we loaded the wounded men in the back. After driving several more miles, in a direction I hoped was away from the front, a group of Japanese halted us, and with threats of shooting us, ordered the truck off the road. They then confiscated the truck and had us remove the wounded men. We placed them in the shade. An American medical officer, hobbling slowly with the other soldiers, stopped and took over. Fortunately there were no guards about.

I was now on foot, and again part of the Death March.

U.S. troops, ravaged by their 28-day besiegement, march off Corregidor to cruel interment, passing fresh Japanese troops on their way to battle.

Chapter 10

THE DEATH MARCH

---◆---

Our life was but a battle and a march
And like the wind's blast, never-resting, homeless
We stormed across the war-convulsed heath.
— *Friedrich Von Schiller*

The dust that enveloped the road was being stirred up by the wheels of trucks and big guns on their way to the front. American and Filipino soldiers emerged through the pall of smoke and dust in endless lines and groups of suffering humanity.

Many suffered from dysentery, and in answering nature's call, ran to the side of the road. Guards kicked at them and pounded them with rifle butts and ordered them back in line. Human forms writhed in the hot dust of the road, and the further we trod, hungry and disillusioned, the number of dead increased proportionally. We stumbled over bodies, the dying and the dead. They lay on both sides of the road and soon became commonplace to us.

I was in a state of shock and not able to pay much attention to what went on around me. It's amazing how our minds are able to adjust to shock. I do, however, remember some things quite vividly, like the incident where a squat Japanese guard with a fixed bayonet saw a soldier at the side of the road with his pants down. The guard grinned and then ran his bayonet into the poor man's behind. Maybe I remember the incident so well because I can't ever forget the grin on the guard's face.

The second day we marched into the night. We had no food nor water, and none was offered, but we were thankful of the chance to lie down and rest.

A few days after I joined ranks in the march, we came to a halt in a village that had been demolished by bombs. Some Filipinos were still living there, and when the guards weren't watching they passed some food to us. Their kindness touched me. I took the chance and approached an older man and asked if he would keep my diary and return it to me after the war. It was a risk but I had little choice. I was certain sooner or later the guards would find it on me and I would be executed on the spot. The old man looked around and nodded that he would do as I asked. I hastily jotted down my name and address and handed it to him. No one saw the transaction. As we prepared to move on I saw him standing in the crowd and wanted to wave to him but dared not. He could have been shot for abetting a prisoner.

The days dragged into weeks. The air was foul with the odor of death. At night we fell asleep where we dropped, and in the mornings we were awakened by outbursts of yelling and screeching. The Japanese guards charged in among us, kicking us to our feet. They then herded us back to the road and started us marching. Walking was torture. Now and again we passed the huddled forms of men who had collapsed from fatigue or had been bayoneted.

Our thirst had become almost unbearable by now. Sometimes one of us was permitted to collect canteens from our comrades and fill them at a stagnant carabao wallows. We held our noses and we drank whatever water we could get.

Prisoners continued to drop, and guards continued their brutal display. There was little we could do for the fallen, except encourage them on. We had learned soon enough that efforts to assist them served only to hasten their deaths and perhaps our own as well. All we could do was encourage them with words. "Don't give up; we're almost there," became our bywords.

The days dragged by, and many prisoners reached the end of their endurance. They went down not singly but by twos and threes. I shall never forget their groans as they tried desperately to get up again, and always with a beaming Japanese guard standing over them with a fixed bayonet. Those who lay lifeless where they had fallen were the only ones free of sinister Japanese brutality.

Bodies were left where they lay, and the stench grew worse and worse with each mile. Occasionally we heard thumping shots from the rifles of guards bringing up the rear, and each shot meant another straggler was dead.

Grinning Japanese infantrymen herd exhausted Corregidor defenders upon their surrender after four months' bitter battle.

U.S. prisoners in the Philippines in captured Japanese photo.

Chapter 11

CAMP O'DONNELL

————•◆•————

One year and two months after I had enlisted in the United States Army, and twenty days after our surrender to the Japanese, we arrived at the rail junction at San Fernando. From here many prisoners were taken by rail to Capas and then marched the final eight miles to our destination, Camp O'Donnell. There was not room on the train for everyone and some of us walked the whole distance. We had marched fifty-five miles on foot, for twenty days, and we left some 10,000 men behind, rotting by the roadside under a tropical sun. For every mile we walked, nearly 180 men lost their lives. Often on the march I wondered if my family had any idea what was happening to us? Did they know I was alive?

Camp O'Donnell wasn't the haven we had hoped for. The place turned out to be a group of dismal, unfinished army buildings. As the men struggled in from the march, the living dead, they collapsed in heaps and lay huddled together on the wooden floors. Some crawled under the buildings and lay on the ground. The Japanese made no attempt to relieve our suffering or to organize the camp. Japanese soldiers, except the guards, stayed away from our area, fearful of contracting dysentery and other diseases from their infected prisoners of war. We were given no food or water until the next day.

We began to organize ourselves, the only way we could survive. We put together makeshift kitchens. The Japanese allowed two servings a day consisting of a small portion of boiled rice in the morning and another equally small portion of steamed rice in the evening. A faucet in the middle of camp provided our water supply. Even our water supply was inadequate. Long lines formed to fill canteens.

During the night, the moans and cries for help were dreadful. Each morning we collected the dead from in and under the buildings. Bodies in twisted forms were placed on litters; it took four men to carry each litter on their shoulders to the graveyard. The dead were dumped in a hole dug the night before. Funeral processions were simple, maybe a few words, and usually took place in the morning.

Camp O'Donnell was infested with hordes of ugly green blowflies. They swarmed by the hundreds on the fecal matter in our latrines, and over the bodies of our dead. They became our curse. We fought them constantly as they attacked our open wounds and our food. We were aware of the deadly germs they carried and did everything possible to keep them away. Often that was impossible. When we received our rice rations, it was already swarming with flies. It was difficult to avoid getting flies into our mouths when we ate. Every spoonful of rice held in my right hand on its way to my mouth had to be accompanied by the frantic waving of my left hand to keep the flies away.

The presence of the green blowflies, as bad as it was, did not compare with the serious threat posed by anopheles, the malaria mosquito. There were very few blankets or mosquito nets available. Those prisoners without nets had no protection from dive-bombing forays at night. Nor did we have quinine or Atabrine to be used for the prevention or treatment of the disease.

Many men became stricken with cerebral malaria, the worst kind, and lacking the necessary medical treatment, died a most horrible death. Constantly throughout the night low moans came from their parched throats and their bodies shook incessantly as they lay naked in pools of their own excreta. We spent endless time trying to force water down their throats. But without quinine or Atabrine, the infected men seldom lasted more than three or four days. They died with white froth on their lips and their arms folded across their chests.

In one of the officers' buildings, I remember seeing a man stretched out on the floor dying. The odor emitted from his body, while he was still alive, was wretched. His flesh was a yellow ashen color. We watched him die, and within fifteen minutes after his death, the smell permeated the entire area. Everyone shouted for his immediate removal. We didn't wait until morning; he was buried in a hurry.

I met one man who, after getting to know him, became a good friend. We had a lot in common and during the day we spent our idle time together talking about and comparing our lives back home. At night we all slept jammed together on the floor, and he always slept next to me. I enjoyed our talks, for I always fell asleep with pleasant thoughts of home on my mind. One morning I awoke to find my head resting on his shoulder. I tried to awaken him only to find that he had died silently and peacefully during the night. No more conversations, no more words. He was dead, gone. After that experience, I avoided sleeping in areas where the men were packed together on the floor.

I remember another night in particular. The monsoons had begun and it was raining heavily. Lightning flashed across the sky and thunder shook the buildings. Wanting to get away from the others, I crawled out on a porch that was partially roofed and squeezing myself against the wall, tried to sleep. I began imagining things. One must wonder what a man's thoughts are at a time like this. Sometimes a bit crazy. That time I pictured myself as a mongrel dog back home in San Francisco, with his tail between his legs, sneaking around in the rain looking for a place to lie down.

I remember too when I had welcomed rain and bad weather back home. That was at Shelter Cove where I worked during the summer months. When the weather made fishing impossible and there was no tanbark to process, we roamed the Shelter Cove Ranch on horseback. Charles and Dorothy East, who operated the ranch for Dorothy's father, William Notley, let us use their horses. We frequently had barnyard rodeos. These were exciting. We took turns trying to ride untamed yearling bulls, while the idle fishing crews and other bystanders enjoyed our attempts to stay on the young bull's bucking backs.

But the monsoon rains were never welcome in prison camp. I had always thought that when men were caught in a life-and-death struggle such as this they would band together to help each other. I found that under the circumstances as they existed at Camp O'Donnell it was just the opposite. The men, to a great extent, became selfish and animalistic. For example, if a man had money, he could buy a little medicine, which might possibly save his life. On the other hand, if a dying man had no money, no matter how much he pleaded, the black marketeer with medicine would walk past him and pay no attention to his condition.

We came to recognize "blackouts" as a serious symptom of various deadly diseases that affected the camp. Many victims of these blackouts swayed back and forth on their feet, and sometimes bounced up and down like rubber balls. As their knees began to buckle, they would start to fall, but then before they hit the ground, they were somehow able to suddenly bounce up again. It was sad to see and yet almost comical to watch.

My first series of blackouts began one day after attacks of both malaria and dysentery had weakened me. I thought death was near and that I would follow the others who had died before me. If I did, I decided I would leave this world in a blaze of glory. I would spend the rest of my days providing all possible help to those who were worse off than I was. I spent all my time consoling the dying and making them more comfortable. Looking back on this time, I now know that the efforts I put forth for others sustained me throughout my interment as a prisoner of war. If I had lain down all day, like many had done, and felt sorry for myself, I would not have survived. Keeping busy and keeping my mind occupied on things other than dying was my secret.

We had occasional inspections by Japanese officers. They strode through camp with surgical masks on their faces to protect them from the foul air and contagious diseases. Other than their quick walk through the camp, they did very little to improve conditions. We were averaging sixty deaths each day. Across the road, Filipino prisoners were interned under similar conditions. According to reports, Filipinos had little resistance to disease and, as a result, as many as several hundred soldiers were dying every day.

Saint Peter's Ward was the name given to the ward set aside for men who were goners, prisoners with no hope for recovery. The men in this ward lay dying and naked, stripped of their clothing which had become saturated with their own excreta. They lay on the hard floor with their heads to the wall. A five gallon can was placed in the middle of the room to be used as a latrine. The can was unnecessary. The men did not have the strength to reach it. There was little or no water to clean the floors and the stench was indescribable. The only part of their bodies that seemed to be alive were their eyes. They were fixed, mostly, on the five gallon can.

Saint Peter's held over thirty patents, and every morning we had to take at least ten, sometimes twenty, who had died in the night, to the graveyard. They were victims not only of tropical diseases, mainly dysentery and malaria, but of malnutrition as well. Starvation was becoming a critical concern. We felt the Japanese intended to let us all die, and thus settle of the problem of caring for their prisoners-of-war. They had to account to no one. They could beat us to death, or starve us to death, and it didn't matter, even to their superior and high ranking officers.

On June 2, 1942, Japanese soldiers suddenly charged through camp, kicking and butting everyone with rifles, yelling and shouting, ordering us to break camp. We didn't know at first if we were to be moved to a new location or exterminated once and for all.

The guards then force marched us to the railroad junction, where we were herded and jammed into freight cars. The train moved slowly, and through openings in the bars we saw Filipinos in the barrios, lining the track, heads bowed, their hand cupped in prayers. We had to stop often, and when we did, Filipinos did their best to toss food to us. The guards' rifle butts stopped us from reaching out. Little food got to us but I will never lose my love and admiration for the Filipino people for how hard they tried to help us. Their loyalty to the American soldiers and the United States never faltered.

The rumor spread that we were going to a camp in Cabanatuan farther to the north. Any camp had to be better than Camp O'Donnell. As I sat jammed in the freight car, pushed far to the rear with my back against the wall, I thought about another move I had once made— when I was a small boy.

I could see it all so clearly. Mama announced one day that we were moving. It was that simple, we were moving. She shooed us out into the street, all seven of us, excluding the baby. The van arrived and the movers began carrying out our furniture and belongings packed in boxes.

Our old home was located on Powell Street in the North Beach District of San Francisco. In a frenzy of excitement, we children stood in the street screaming, hopping up and down, pushing one another with excitement. Attracted by our antics, all the boys and girls on the block had swarmed around to witness our departure.

Suddenly a Model T Ford zoomed around the corner, bounced along the cobblestones, and came to rest at the curb. And who could it be to step out but Papa. As I sat in the dark in that frightfully crowded freight car, rumbling through Filipino countryside to an uncertain destination, I could clearly visualize Papa that day as he had opened the door and stepped out like a conquering hero. The ovation we gave him would have pleased Caesar entering the Coliseum in his chariot.

It almost seemed that I was there and that it was happening all over again. Mama and the baby took seats in the front seat of the Model T while the other seven kids and I crammed into the back. Papa drove us past the marina and through the Presidio to avoid traffic. As we rumbled down the streets of San Francisco, people stopped to stare; some shook their heads; others waved gleefully. We left the Presidio, tore down the Arguello Street Hill and, as we neared the bottom, a sharp report rang out and the Ford began to shake violently. Papa didn't slow down. He informed us it was only a flat tire and it was useless to stop and change it since we had only a few blocks to go to our new home.

Clanking loudly and bouncing up and down, the Model T and its jolly passengers limped up to its destination. Papa opened the doors and we scrambled out onto the sidewalk. Looking up and down the street, I was amazed to see the houses were jammed together—rowhouses they were—and that all the roofs were sharply pointed. Before us stood a large two-story home. What happy memories the very thought of that old house brought to my mind! Unbeknown to us, Papa had built our living quarters in the basement, with bedrooms above.

The heat in the freight car became unbearable. San Francisco was never this hot, I thought. I remembered now, how during the holidays, Nonno and Nonna, our grandfather and grandmother, would spend a few days with us. Nonno was eighty years old at the time. He had a bushy blond mustache and blue eyes. As a young man he had fished in the Mediterranean Sea and served in the Italian army. When he and Papa arrived in San Francisco, they fished the waters of the bay. One year they went to Alaska and spent the season fishing for salmon, where Nonno's catch for that particular season was the highest ever caught. His first name was Gaetano and as he was the first man from his community in Sicily to come to America. He was called Gaetano-Americano. At eighty years of age, he loved to fence with me. I was then about six years old. Brandishing yardsticks, we would cross swords and Nonno would have his hands full as I darted in and out between his legs.

Nonno was also a wonderful storyteller. I remember so well those stories. Every evening we would sit around the stove. With a twinkle in his eye and a twist of his moustache, he'd tell a story in his fine Italian. Two of his favorites were "The Count of Monte Cristo" and "Ali Baba and the Forty Thieves." He also related many humorous stories that would hold us spellbound at first and then send us into hysterics.

Memories, how they can keep us alive. Our life in the basement had been a happy one, and it was these pleasant thoughts that came back to me aboard the prison train. Throughout the time in prison my greatest force of resistance was my mother's image, which always appeared to me when I was ill with fever or near death. She had been born in Italy and had not had one day of schooling. She could not speak English; we learned to converse in Italian. She died when I was seventeen. She had a simple childlike faith and a great love for her family.

Beautiful thoughts came interrupted with reality. A prisoner began pounding his head against the side of the rail car, shouting as he did, demanding to know when the war would end. We had no news, no word from the outside world. All we had were rumors, and more rumors.

In one month we had left over 1,500 dead at Camp O'Donnell.

Chapter 12

CABANATUAN

——◆——

On June 2, 1942, we arrived at Camp Cabanatuan, a prison of war camp for both Filipinos and Americans. What we hoped for the better turned out for the worse. Although it was much larger and had more buildings than Camp O'Donnell, it lacked even the basic essentials. There were no kitchens nor even latrines. And it was completely disorganized. The Japanese simply dumped us inside the gates and turned away. Even their guards failed to provide proper security.

A few men took advantage of the weak security. They had the nerve to sneak out of the camp at night and buy food from the Filipinos. They did this not once but several times. One night, however, Japanese guards caught them sneaking back into the camp. They were taken to headquarters, tied to posts, and beaten intermittently over the next few days. Finally, one morning we were all called out and told to line up. Soon a squad of Japanese soldiers appeared, leading the men. The prisoners with their hands tied behind their backs were lined up before us. A firing squad took its position. An officer gave the order and a volley of shots tore through their bodies. The officer then fired his pistol into each body to make sure every man was dead.

After this incident, Japanese headquarters announced that all prisoners of war would be organized into groups of ten. Every man was assigned to one of these groups. If one man of the group escaped, the other nine would be shot. If a group of ten escaped, nine other groups would face death. There were very few who tried to escape, knowing that they would endanger the lives of other men.

During the first days at Cabanatuan, the food served us was wretched. It came out of poorly equipped makeshift kitchens, was badly prepared and barely provided enough calories to keep us alive. Occasionally we did have a half canteen of greens, but very little meat. Once a week we each had a ladle of carabao soup, served from five gallon cans. If we were lucky, we might get a piece of meat the size of our fingernail with our soup. If the server had a friend in the line and served him from the bottom of the can, his friend would get several pieces of meat. Such favoritism led to arguments and always ended with bad feelings among the prisoners.

Rice that had a strong moldy taste was our main dish, and often our only dish. We had boiled rice in the morning and steamed rice in the evening. It came mixed with bits of rocks, sand, weevils, grubs and rat filth. It was so unclean it was hard to distinguish between a grain of rice and a grub. Most of us felt that it was useless to try to separate the rice from the grubs. We often kidded each other that the weevils and grubs were loaded with protein. I think we wanted to believe that.

One man in my building was a chronic complainer about the food. He took issue with the moldy taste of the rice, the grubs and the weevils. According to him, the food was not fit for pigs. We all agreed with him, but what could we do? Complaining wouldn't help. We encouraged the man who complained to eat his food, just to survive. He refused to listen to our pleas. Eventually he lost his appetite, contracted dysentery, and was moved to another building.

About a month later, I was sent to the same building to help with the sick. There on a nearby bunk was the complainer, the man who wouldn't eat. His eyes were sunken deep in their sockets and his face was distorted. He was lying on his side with his legs bent at the knees in a fixed position, and his back curved outward. He had lain in that position for so long that his back and his knees had become stiff. It was impossible to get him into a flat position. We gently tried to straighten his legs and back, but the pain was so great we discontinued our efforts. In a few days he was dead. He was nothing but a rack of bones covered with skin. This was one of the worst cases of malnutrition that I encountered during my stay in camp.

Another man, whose name was Wolfe, we called the Human Sump. At chow time he would wander around looking for men who were too sick to eat. The grubs, weevils, rat filth, the moldy taste in the rice, all this had no effect on his appetite. He would plead with sick men to give him their ration of rice. This man was well known and recognized by everyone as he made his daily appearance around the camp. His stomach was swollen, partly from all the garbage he ate, and partly from malnutrition. He too eventually died.

As time went by, we organized our prison life more efficiently. We set aside a hospital area of thirty-three large army barracks capable of holding approximately 100 men per building. These barracks were numbered 0 to 32. Ward 0 was the death ward. We segregated the other buildings according to the different malnutrition-related diseases.

The buildings were similar in size, shape and even appearance to Pullman cars. They were long with a walkway down the middle. The areas on each side of the walkway were constructed of bamboo slats. You could see the ground through the openings where the slats didn't come together. Ladders led to an upper deck with a floor also made of bamboo slats. There were no separate rooms and the men slept close together, an equal number on each deck.

The month of June came bringing the monsoons, and monsoons in the tropics mean rains. Rain fell in torrents, day and night, unrelentingly. They were accompanied by fierce flashes of lightning and loud peals of thunder. There was no glass in the windows and those near the openings got soaked during the night as they slept.

My first day as a medic assigned to Ward 1 was most disconcerting. It was pouring down rain in sheets, and as I approached the building to go on duty, a couple men were standing in the rain, naked and shivering violently. I found other men in the nude under the building. I asked them angrily what they were doing out in the rain. They told me that they had been thrown out of the building because they had an attack of dysentery and had messed up the bamboo slats and the walkway.

In a fury I entered the building. I quickly made it clear to all prisoners that no matter how bad a man had dysentery he was entitled to stay in his bunk when it was raining. Cleanup would be made regularly every morning, and between rain squalls when necessary. I was determined that they follow my rule.

Serious arguments that often turned into fist fights arose when a man with an uncontrollable case of dysentery sleeping on an upper deck sprayed the man sleeping below him with excrement. Again, there was little that could be done.

We held sick call routinely every morning. But the only medicine we had to hand out was a little sodium bicarbonate and a few ointments. There was absolutely nothing else available for anyone.

Scabies, those nasty little parasites that burrow into the skin, ran wild throughout the camp. Men continuously scratched, like monkeys. The scratching was worse at night. The only way we could eliminate the bug was to boil clothing, but that only helped for a short time. The itch always returned and we learned that scabies, the seven year itch as we called it, was something we simply had to live with. At least it didn't kill.

The men in Ward 0 suffered from advanced stages of malaria, dysentery and various malnutrition-related diseases. Ward 1, to which I had been assigned, was next door to Ward O and I had frequent opportunity to observe what happened in the death ward. Unlike most of the structures, Ward 0 consisted of one large room with a solid wooden floor. As in St. Peter's ward at Camp O'Donnell, the men were laid close together on the floor with their heads to the wall. As many as forty living skeletons lay naked in pools of excreta waiting to die. Nothing could be done for them. They were seriously ill and doomed to death. Without medicine, we were unable to help them. We couldn't offer them blankets, or even a dry place to lie down.

Each morning we'd find that twenty-five or more of the forty men confined to Ward 0 had died of either the lack of medicine or from the cold the night before. When the ward personnel came to work, they would carry the bodies out and pile them on the gravel to await burial. Those who remained alive would then be carried outside by the arms and legs and placed on the ground, and not always gently. The attendants used squeegees to push the urine and fecal matter out the door, except for the filth that was stuck to the wood and couldn't be moved. Our water supply was inadequate to get rid of all of the mess. Flies were everywhere, on the floors, the walls, and all over the bodies of the living as well as the dead who awaited burial.

I remember one man in Ward 0 who refused to give up. He was determined he wasn't going to die. This man had more courage and fortitude than any one person I have ever known. One morning, on my way to work, I passed Ward 0, and as the living and the dead were being carried out of the building, a weak voice called to me. I turned in the direction of voice, and there I saw a sight so revolting that I gasped and fell back for a second. Before me was a human skeleton lying on the ground, looking up at me. His features were greatly distorted. His nose was pushed to one side; his eyes sunken; his skin like paste. I could have been looking at Frankenstein's monster. The poor fellow could not have weighed more than seventy pounds. Feebly he reached out a hand, and then in no more than a whisper he called, "Mario, Mario."

I fell back farther. I studied the face. The eyes, something about the eyes. I remembered now. I had spoken to this man often at Camp O'Donnell.

"Help me, Mario, help me," he called again, in a voice hardly audible.

I bent over him and put a hand under his shoulder for support. "What is it?" I asked. What meaningless words to ask a dying man, for I had no medicine, no blankets, no food that I could give him. But he didn't ask for any of these. He asked for salt. "Salt?" I asked in dismay.

"Yes, a little salt," he repeated. He then explained, in words that did not come easy, that if he had a little salt, he might be able to eat some rice. I assured him that I would do everything possible to help him.

That afternoon I contacted a friend who worked in the kitchen. "Not much," I said, "just a pinch. He gave me a small bag of salt and the next morning I gave this to the dying man in Ward 0. He didn't have to thank me; his eyes showed his gratitude. I kept the supply of salt coming, and each morning he seemed a little stronger. I was able to spend some time with him. We had conversations either inside Ward 0 or outside on the ground where he lay while the ward was cleaned up. Miraculously, for more than four months, he had survived the horrors of Ward 0. I cannot even begin to estimate how many men I had seen carried out of that dreadful place, and each morning when I arrived I didn't know if I would see my friend lying on the ground or else heaped up among the dead waiting to be carried to the cemetery.

But he was always there.

After another two months in Ward 0, a total of six months altogether, the man finally managed to get on his feet, and slowly he got better. By sheer determination to live, he continued to improve until he finally was dismissed from the hospital and assigned work on the farm. But his first day on the farm proved to be too hard for him. They carried him back on a stretcher and placed him in Ward 0 again, naked, and with his head against the wall. He endured the impossible conditions of the ward for another month. Then one morning, he was gone. I was certain he was dead, but when I inquired if he had already been buried, they informed me he was still alive. But he had contacted another disease. They had carried him to the tuberculosis ward. He now had another battle to fight.

I was at Cabanatuan about three months when I began to have trouble urinating. I had the urge to urinate, but the only liquid I could pass was a few drops of blood, accompanied by much pain. I went to sick call. The medical officer examined me but all he could do was shake his head. That was the extent of his ability to help me cope with my problem. My thoughts focused on Ward 0 and death. I wouldn't let that happen. In two weeks my urination became normal. Much the same happened with my battle with malaria. I had it bad and continued to have attacks. There was no quinine or Atabrine to help me, and all I could do was let the fever run its course. Somehow it always worked. I never ever knew how sick I really was until my comrades told me afterwards. They said that I jabbered like I had gone insane. There was nothing anyone could have done to help me anyway. Help had to come from within me. I can't explain it, and I don't think any medical scientist can either—but it did work

I tried not to think of death but sometimes it was unavoidable. At times our subconscious thoughts and even our dreams take over and we have no control. I am back in San Francisco with a gang of boys, romping around in the Odd Fellows Cemetery.

Anyone who is observant and strolls down Geary Boulevard in San Francisco can't help from pausing at Jordan Avenue and marveling at the domed structure that stands at this most unnatural setting. The doomed building is a columbarium, and over years it witnessed the changes that came to the area. Once the cemetery stretched from the foot of Cross Hill to Arguello Boulevard on the west, and from Turk Street on the south to Geary Boulevard, near our family home. The Odd Fellows Cemetery back then was enclosed in some sections by a concrete wall, and in others by board fences.

When we first moved to our new neighborhood, we listened with awe to the many tales people had to tell about the graveyard. For us youngsters, Old Fellows became a place of mystery and intrigue, and each one of us hesitated to venture near the place. Our parents cautioned us to keep out of the place.

But in time our curiosity overcame our fear. The day arrived when we mustered up enough courage to cross Arguello Boulevard and have a look for ourselves. Peeking through knotholes in the fence, we were amazed and fascinated by the scene before us. High grass, tangled bushes, tall trees, and tombstone of all inscriptions blend to form what appeared to be a wild enchanted forest.

Finding a hole in the fence, we cautiously crawled through and commenced to explore a small area. We left the cemetery feeling confident now. A few days later we returned, and explored a bit farther. After that we became bolder, and soon we knew every corner of the entire cemetery.

How clearly at night in camp I could recall that cemetery. In the center stood a large crematorium. Its windows and doors were barred, and on the east side of the structure towered a square, concrete chimney. Looking down through gratings, we could see a murky abyss and occasionally we caught the glimpse of a rat or snake stirring in its depths. The building had a sinister aspect, and we were afraid to venture too close.

During our explorations, we peeked into open tombs, climbed trees, crawled under bushes. We wondered about different statues, and read names and dates on the graves. We discovered that the bushes made excellent hideouts and the trees and tombstones gave us a good view of the surrounding area. The grounds abounded with all sort of wildlife: quail, robins, woodpeckers, sparrows, and many other species of birds. There were also garter snakes, and, we learned, a few vicious caretakers.

I remembered one day we entered the cemetery and saw a caretaker cleaning up around the graves. Everyone wanted to dash out into the street again before we pounced upon us.

"Now listen, you guys," I said, being the wise one. "What are you afraid of? Have we done anything wrong?"

"Nope," answered a little fellow, "but I'm not taking any chances."

I took up the challenge. "Well," I relied boldly, "if he comes up here, I'm staying."

About then the caretaker saw us, and leaving his work, he dropped his shovel and rapidly strode toward us. Immediately, the gang scrambled to the fence and disappeared through the opening. I stood fast, acting nonchalant, as if I had done nothing wrong. He walked up to me, grabbed my arm and swung me around. He then booted me twice in the seat of the pants and gave me a shove toward the fence.

"Get the hell outa here, you squirt," he shouted in anger. Tears rolled down my cheeks. Between sobs, I cried, "Just wait till I tell my father. He's bigger than you are!"

Greatly chagrined, I hurried back to the street. Some of the gang had heard what I had said, about my father being bigger than the caretaker, and they began laughing and teasing me. I was so angry I wanted to fight the whole bunch.

My standing up to the caretaker paid off. He became sympathetic. On Memorial Day he paid us to clean the graves. Our pay was fifty cents for a single grave, one dollar for a double and as high as five dollars for multiple plots. I can still hear our cries as we walked through the cemetery shouting: "Graves cleaned and watered." We sometimes made fifteen dollars apiece on grave cleaning days.

At Cabanatuan the Japanese allowed us to have a service on Memorial Day. The whole camp crowded around the graveyard where we conducted our own ceremonies. I was most impressed by the service given by a member of the Jewish faith. The man was about sixty years of age, over six feet tall, and had a big bushy beard. He resembled a portrait of Moses. He was deeply tanned and his only clothing was a tattered pair of shorts. In a deep resounding voice he sang his service. We all were deeply affected by his presentation. When the time came for the bugler to blow taps, he was usually so overcome with emotion that he could hardly blow his horn.

Every time I gazed out over the graveyard, I couldn't help thinking of our many dead buried there. They had suffered greatly, needlessly, and with as many as twenty or thirty at a time dumped in a common hole, they could truthfully be called "unknown soldiers." Their bodies could never be identified.

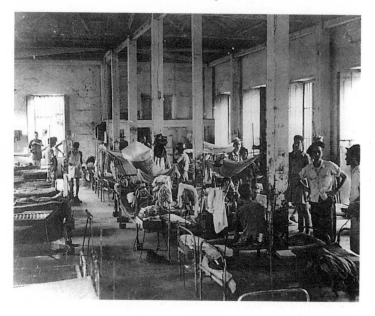

A Prison "Hospital.".

Chapter 13

INMATES TO THE LAST

———◆——

The rainy season posed a serious problem for burying our dead. The drainage was very poor and some bodies became exposed each time it rained. It was difficult, if not impossible, to cover them when the earth had turned into mud. Often we could hear dogs howling at night, and some of us were convinced that these wild animals were eating our dead.

A new patient came to the ward one day with an unusually large amount of clothing. He had several pairs of Khaki pants, a few shirts, three pairs of shoes and other bits and pieces. We didn't know how he had acquired it all, but in a week's time, everything he owned had disappeared. It was stolen during the night as he lay asleep.

During the man's short stay in the ward, he developed a close friendship with another man who slept beside him. As I walked up and down the aisle, I noticed that they often rested with their heads on each other's arms. They had apparently found solace in each other's company. After just a few days in the ward, the man who had so much clothing died of unknown symptoms. His friend followed him two days later.

Homosexuality was not common in the camp. There were a few gay soldiers, but the weakened condition of the men held any sexual activity to a minimum. Nevertheless, it did exist. I remembered one incident involving a gay sergeant and a Japanese soldier. My barracks was next to a Japanese post and we had to bow or salute the guards as we walked past. This gay sergeant always make a bow that appeared to be curtsy and the Japanese soldiers were impressed with his manner. One day, as I happened to be in the barracks with a bout of malaria, I noticed the sergeant resting on the floor when a Japanese soldier entered and flashed some bills in front him. The sergeant and the Japanese left, and we suspected that was the start or their relationship.

Thievery was common and wide spread in the prison camp. There was no place to hide anything. Even as a man lay dying, whatever clothing he was wearing would disappear during the night. In the morning, the dead man would be naked, ready for the graveyard in the same condition he came into the world.

Scurvy, caused by the lack of vitamins, was a serious threat to everyone. We all suffered greatly from the disease. At times my tongue was so swollen I could hardly swallow. My gums bled and my teeth became loose and came near to falling out. Many men did lose their teeth.

The worst threat was diphtheria, and when it suddenly made its appearance in camp, we were really scared. We immediately erected a huge tent that could house a hundred men at a time. Here we isolated patients with the dreaded disease. It seemed to do little good. In no time at all the tent was filled with ailing men. We had no antitoxin or medication to fight the disease. As the number of dead began to mount, each man waited in fear that he would be the next to go.

Sleeping as close together as we had to in such confined quarters in the barracks, it was impossible not to ignore the man next to you. If you didn't like your neighbor, you could move away providing you could find space somewhere else to lie down. You always moved if you thought the person next to you had a contagious disease. But moving from one place to another was no assurance you were better off.

I had one neighbor, a Dutchman, I came to like very much. We used to lie awake at night and talk about the future. He was very much interested in the delicatessen business, and so he spent much time telling me how he prepared different kinds of sausages and jars of pickles. Our talking about the future seemed to keep him, and me, from facing reality in Cabanatuan.

We had to sleep so close together that we often breathed in each other's face during the night. One afternoon when I returned from the ward he was missing. I asked where he had gone, and was told he had contracted diphtheria and had been taken to the isolation tent.

I visited him a few days later. From a distance I tried to talk to him. He was unable to eat, and he motioned to me that he was having a hard time swallowing and breathing. We decided that if he were to survive he needed some kind of tube or straw to breathe through. A friend in surgery gave me a pipette, a glass tube used in a laboratory. I was so pleased that I could help my friend that I rushed back to the tent to give it to him. I was too late. I found him dead. I felt myself grow weak and I broke into a sweat. I knew I had been exposed to the same bug that caused his death. Yet somehow I was spared.

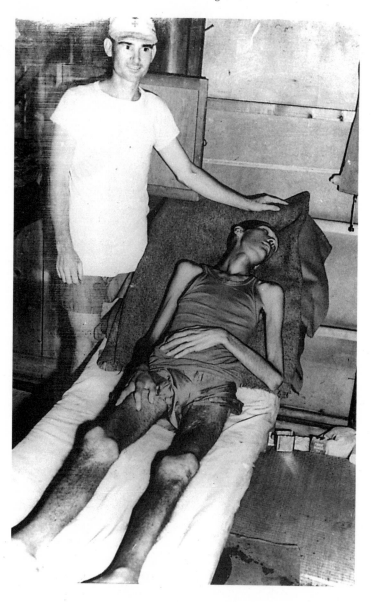

A gaunt U.S. prisoner of war.

Chapter 14

THE PRISONER
FROM SHELTER COVE

One day, upon checking the roster in one of the wards, I thought I recognized the name of a fisherman who had spent his summers in Shelter Cove. I was excited at the possibility of seeing someone I had known from back home. I planned to look him up the next day.

I did and found him in the ward. He immediately remembered me. We talked the whole day about our mutual friends and experiences we had shared at the cove. He reminded me how his father, like mine, had fished the area for many years. He seemed very happy, not with his lot, but that he had survived diphtheria and been dismissed from the tent a few short days before I met him. He was now recuperating in another ward.

In the days that followed, we spent many hours together talking about the cove and the people we knew. We talked about going out for salmon, and the fog suddenly rolling in, and the times the sea got bad and how some boats had a tough time returning to shore. Our conversations were punctuated with "remember the time" and on and on we'd go. What was so rewarding for us both was the pleasure we had in finding someone in camp from back home. After his bout with death he seemed to have recovered remarkably. I came to see him one afternoon, excited about a friend I had remembered and was anxious to see if he too knew him. He greeted me warmly, as he always did, but as I began to talk his eyes suddenly got a faraway look, as if he were looking far across the oceans, and then, without warning he collapsed. He stopped breathing. We did all we could to revive him, but our efforts failed. The doctor on the ward explained that he had died of paralysis caused by diphtheria. Many of those who had contacted diphtheria and did survive later developed paralysis as an after effect.

The loss of this newly discovered friend made me realize how impossible it was for friendships to last under these conditions. No one was ever sure that he'd live to see another day.

The diphtheria plague raged through the prison camp like a grass fire out of control. It became so serious that a group of Japanese officers finally came for an inspection. What they saw was a pitiful sight, hundreds upon hundreds of prisoners dying. The officers just stood there, in their neat uniforms, sabres hanging at their sides, when a doctor suddenly appeared and placed himself directly in front of the officer in charge of the inspection party. He was fearless, and under other circumstances his action could have led to a severe beating or even his death. "I demand," he shouted out, within hearing distance of everyone around, "I demand that we receive medical aid immediately." The officer was obviously astonished and taken back by this sudden outburst, but what the doctor had to say next threw him further off guard. "I am a medical doctor and I know this disease. If we do not receive help, the whole camp will die, everyone, including Japanese soldiers and not only those guarding us. The disease will kill all Japanese as well. It can become a plague that has no bounds!"

He made an impression. Within a few days the antitoxin we needed to combat the disease arrived in camp. Every prisoner was immediately inoculated and the menace of diphtheria was lessened.

The short friendship with my friend from Shelter Cove brought back many fond memories of home. It was as though he opened a flood gate and every night when I lay down to sleep my thoughts turned to Shelter Cove.

The thought of this beautiful secluded spot helped me forget the death and suffering around me. It also helped to sustain me at this time. It gave me something to hang on to, something to remember.

I would close my eyes, putting the horrible reality of Cabanatuan out of my mind, and again I would be walking from the dock to the hotel. I had arrived aboard International No. 3 to work for the summer. In my mind I could so clearly see the faces of my brother Tony and Sal Russo, the company manager. They were there to greet me. They led me to the hotel, talking all the way about the good fishing, and showed me my room. The window opened out to the cove, and I could hear seagulls calling. They then anxiously showed me around the area. What a delightful little spot.

Next to the hotel was a small grocery store. "Long ago the building was a trading post," Sal said pointing out the structure to me. A little farther on we came to another spacious building. "This was the barn when horses were used to cross over the mountains to Garberville," he continued. Sal pointed to the blacksmith shop that was still there, but now instead of horse stalls there was a large garage, a cooking shack and living quarters for those who worked there. There were also two large tanbark sheds.

The company had five head of yearling calves and two cows which were milked twice daily, some chickens and a hay field.

Tony was the engineer for the company. He was responsible for the refrigeration and ice machine, the saltwater pumps, and the tanbark engine.

I was introduced to the crew. Strange that I could remember all their names, and what names. There was Vince Argento, Toni Davi, Bradley Radcliffe, Charlie Farnsworth and Slim Knapp. Slim was the caretaker; Salvatore Pizzimenti was the salmon splitter.

The pier at that time was used to unload salmon from the small boats for processing in the fishhouse. I had been given the job of helping to unload the boats at the end of the dock and to push the boxes of salmon into the plant, where they were cleaned and iced. It was common to unload sixty or seventy boats during a day, and the job might last until ten or eleven o'clock at night. All the salmon were shipped by drag boat to San Francisco.

Our mornings we spent preparing the large salmon for mild curing. Salvatore Pizzimenti, the salmon splitter, would slice the big fish and take the backbone out. The fish were then dipped into the brine and salted in barrels.

Besides the San Francisco International Fish Company, there were several other companies with short-term storage barges anchored in the cove receiving fish. Pick-up boats carried the fish from barges to Fort Bragg, where they emptied their load and returned for more. The largest total daily catch that I could remember was 140,000 pounds. What relief a mere tenth of those fish could bring to our sick and starving men at Cabanatuan!

Fishing boat crews dreaded the winds that came from the northwest. When they blew, the boats were unable to fish and the men were put to work in the tanbark sheds. During July, the tan oak trees were cut and the bark peeled and stored in the sheds until it dried. After it was processed, it was used to tan leather and fish nets.

Some individuals stuck in my mind more than others. One was Charlie Farnsworth. I used to wonder what he would do if the Japanese had him in camp. He was a no nonsense man. Charlie was a truck driver, and I had the pleasure of working with him. He was also my teacher. He was a skilled woodsman and an expert hunter, and he taught me how to use an axe and how to hunt deer. Charlie was about sixty-two then, and I would wonder if he still might be alive. How I missed Charlie.

There were amusing times at Shelter Cove, and recalling these moments made me chuckle to myself. There was the time they wouldn't let us in the hotel and we had to eat outside. They had good reason. We had spent the day cutting hay, getting it ready for storing in the barn. All was going well until the hay mower cut through some skunk holes. A couple skunks dashed out running for cover when our dogs grabbed hold them and shook them by the necks. The skunks sprayed the dogs, us and the hay field. We stunk terribly, and nothing could get rid of the smell. It wasn't very pleasant eating dinner outside in the cold.

But then, even on Bataan in the humid tropics it got cold, terribly cold. And the cold seemed to go right through our weakened bodies.

Chapter 15

THE YOUNGEST
PRISONER IN CAMP

In the camp Cabanatuan there was a young boy who was always cold, even when the sun was shining. He was no more than seventeen and had obviously falsified his age to get into the service.

When the boy first appeared in camp, he had very little clothing and he walked around in the nude. Someone felt sorry for him and gave him a heavy woolen army coat that hung to the ground. He wore it day and night, even when the sun was shinning its hottest. We called him Yardbird, and there wasn't anyone who didn't like him. But the poor kid lacked stamina, and the will to continue. We found Yardbird dead one morning, wrapped in his army coat. Even the doctors didn't know why he had died. They say you can't die of fear, and that home sickness doesn't kill you, but I think they're wrong. The boy must have missed his family. We sadly carried him out to the graveyard. Always when we buried our dead, we put them to rest without one stitch of clothing. We buried the boy in his overcoat, and it was the first time no one objected. I thought often about that boy throughout my stay in prison. Why did the Japanese have to take his life away from him? Why do the young have to die for someone else's crimes?

Beriberi also took its toll. It was a common malnutrition disease caused when rice is a major portion of anyone's diet. Beriberi results from a deficiency of thiamine and minerals and in extreme cases can lead to a gradual degeneration of the nerves and even heart failure. The symptoms are an overabundance of fluid in the tissues.

Before the 1800s almost half the sailors of the British and American navies were likely to develop beriberi and many died of it. It was the Japanese who found the cure for beriberi when in 1870 they began adding fish, meat and vegetables to their regular diet, but in spite of this knowledge they did nothing to alleviate beriberi among the prisoners at camp Cabanatuan.

One method we used to check to see if we had beriberi was to push the flesh in our leg inward with the thumb. If an indentation occurred and the flesh remained indented, fluids were present, and we knew we had a form of beriberi. There were many men with advanced cases of the disease scattered around camp. I stopped to talk to one man who sat on the edge of his sleeping pallet. His legs were swollen and his abdomen was so distended that it rested on his thighs. His scrotum was the size of a volleyball. He sat there naked, unable to avoid the filth around him or move or help himself. I wanted to help him but here was nothing I could do. A couple vitamin B capsules or a little meat would have cured him.

The pain caused by beriberi can be excruciating. It affects lower extremities. The men who suffered the most complained about the pain in their feet being unbearable. Some of them could barely walk, and others, who were unable to walk, sat holding their toes all day and most of the night. Sleep was almost impossible for them.

Every other type of tropical disease was found in some form or another in camp. Many men developed ulcers in their intestines; some developed ulcers in their eyes from lack of vitamin A.

Another common malady was "jungle rot." It was dreadful. The inflicted had open sores, some the size of the palms of their hands, that would not heal. The few ointments we had were not effective since the underlying problem with jungle rot was not the lack of vitamins but that of malnutrition, exposure and dysentery. The latter kept our bodies in extremely poor physical condition and susceptible to the rot.

Men with red hair and fair skin suffered the most. They were more vulnerable to skin disorders since they couldn't stand the bright sun on their bodies. And there was no escaping the sun when prisoners had to go on work details.

Many men became victims of their own attitudes, which were reflected in their behavior. They didn't seem to have the will to live, so they lay idly in their bunks day and night. After they had lain for a few weeks with no exercise and with their knees flexed, what muscle they had left became so stiff that they were unable to straighten their legs. They lost their appetites, refused to eat, and in a short time they became racks of bones and died.

We built latrines all around the camp. These were long, narrow, deep ditches covered with benchlike structures that had holes in the top similar to the old outhouses. The benches were not enclosed, but open to the weather. Some had six holes; others had twelve. They were constantly in use day and night. We also had thousands of little red ants that were a nuisance around the camp. They were extremely antagonistic and their bite was painful.

One night at the height of one of my many bouts with dysentery, severe cramps hit me and I rushed outside the barracks and headed for the latrine. The moon was full and I could see several men already sitting on one end of a twelve-holder. I saw little chance for privacy so I ran down to the hole that was farthest from the men already seated. No one was sitting there. Pulling down my shorts, I quickly sat down and let go.

Immediately I came out of the hole like a rocket headed for the moon. I must have leaped several feet in the air, screaming at the top of my lungs. I had sat on a swarm of little ants. They had immediately attacked my buttocks and genitals and were biting me severely. My screams awoke the camp. Men came running out of their barracks to see me jumping around in circles in the moonlight, slapping at my bottom, like some one who had stepped on hot coals. At first they thought I must have flipped my lid, had gone mad. When they did learn what had happened, there was nothing anyone could do. It took me about ten minutes to pluck the ants from my body. I had to make several more trips to the latrine that night, but I didn't mind giving up my privacy to avoid the red ants.

The Japanese never interfered with our religious worship. We had a devoted group of chaplains in camp and they did everything possible to help the men with their problems. Religious services were conducted daily and many prisoners who were able attended. Altars of the various denominations were placed around the camp. The Catholic altar was set up near one of the latrines, and as a result, I was able to attend mass sitting in the latrine. It was to say the least convenient. The location of the altar made it possible not only for me but for any prisoner with dysentery to attend the service. We had the choice of sitting with the group at the altar or on the nearby twelve-holer. Sacrilegious? Maybe, but we were all sure that the Lord was making allowances for our condition.

Often when I attended mass my thoughts wandered back in time to the weekends I spent at Shelter Cove. Sunday morning was always church day, but Saturday nights was the time we would howl. How crystal clear these memories were to me in Camp Cabanatuan. Sometimes I felt I was there in the cove.

We had everything in Shelter Cove we wanted; we didn't have to make the long, bumpy ride to Garberville, the closest town to the cove. The road was very narrow, mountainous and dusty. Sal Russo, the company manager, imported the action to us from town.

Sal would crank the phone and invite everyone in town he could think of to come to our dances Saturday night. The International No. 3 sailed up from Frisco once a week, bringing groceries, meat, fruits, and usually a barrel of wine for our Saturday night parties. This was always a happy event and everyone went to the dock to meet and unload the drag boat.

Our dance orchestra consisted of Mac MacArthur on the violin, Sal Russo strumming the guitar, Salvatore Pizzimenti playing the mandolin and my brother, Tony, squeezing the accordion. We danced to "Over the Waves," dozens of Italian waltzes and endless marches. What fun we had! The dancing lasted until at least two o'clock in the morning. There were many sore, thumping heads in church Sunday mornings.

Chapter 16

CAMP EDIBLES
- RATS, CATS AND DOGS

Among the loot the Japanese had seized after the fall of Bataan were several hundred cases of canned milk. For the 50,000 men interned, the camp was allotted a few cans per day. These we gave to the men who suffered the most from malnutrition. If nothing else, it didn't cure them but it helped keep them alive a bit longer.

Aside from nutrition for the dying, the milk cans had another great importance to our medical staff. The labels were carefully taken off, reversed, and used for keeping records. The Japanese did not issue paper of any sort for our medical staff to use.

The Japanese did allow one group of men in camp a special privilege. The electricians, the men in charge of the camp's electrical system, were given permission to dig pits to trap wild dogs. We could tell when they were successful; we could hear the howls of the wild beasts after they had fallen into the traps. As a result the camp electricians were well-nourished from the protein from the dogs they ate. They were one group who didn't suffer from any malnutrition diseases.

I had the honor of being invited one night to dine with them. I had helped them build a "quan" stove, and the meal they cooked and invited me to share with them was dog meatloaf. It was actually quite good.

I had helped build the quan stove as a project to keep busy. I believed that keeping myself constantly occupied would also go a long way toward keeping my mind busy, and keeping my mind busy might perhaps help me stay alive. I knew I could not dwell upon the suffering going on all around me. Building quan stoves was but sure way to keep busy. It also got me some free meals from time to time.

The stove got its name from the word "quan" we used in camp to refer to food of any description. Quan meant the morning meal, the evening meal, all kinds of food or anything related to food.

We made the stove out of adobe bricks and four 44-gallon gasoline drums. The firebox was exceptionally long. The stove had a grill made from a half drum to cover the top. The half sections of the drum which we didn't use for the quan we used to sterilize mess kits. The other two drums became the ovens. A single fire roared under and over the gasoline drums and serviced the whole stove. We were able to heat water, grill, and bake simultaneously.

The Japanese permitted us to build our quan stoves and allowed us to cook anything we wanted, which meant anything we could find that was edible. Our menus consisted of rats, stray cats, wild dogs, snakes, cockroaches and pig weed. The meals were occasional. Whenever we could catch something, and whatever it happened to be, it was devoured with great pleasure. We eagerly gobbled up everything and anything.

Every time the subject of rats came up in Cabanatuan, my thoughts would revert to my home in North Beach, the Italian district in San Francisco. Our flat was only a few blocks from the waterfront where rats had a field day.

The downstairs in our flat was always heavily laden with the pungent smell of fermenting wine. A spooky alley led from a small yard in the rear of our flat to a parking street in the back. We had to pass dark, damp cellars to reach the street. Huge rats thrived in the farthest recesses of the cellars. Unafraid and defiant, they would scurry up and down the alley during the day, march boldly through the yard, and pass from one flat to another. They held an undisputed reign over the entire basement area, which was never challenged unless an adult descended the stairs to draw wine from a barrel.

Due to the dreaded fear we kids had for rats, we seldom used the alleyway, wine cellars or yard. Never, in a million years, would I have thought back then that I would one day enjoy "rat a la Cabanatuan" as the main course on my dinner table. What the urge to survive can do to one.

Chapter 17

DOWN ON THE FARM

———◆——

As time passed, we managed to organize our camp much better than it was when we first arrived. The Japanese high command decided to allow us to farm some land near camp. For our labor we would get a small portion of what we grew. A little something was better than nothing.

Each morning a large group of physically able men lined up for roll call and then marched to the farm, always closely guarded by soldiers carrying rifles with fixed bayonets.

We spent our days hoeing, planting, moving dirt, and fertilizing the plants with human excrements from the latrines. In time we grew and harvested okra, camote, corn, cabbage, rice and cassava. Almost all the produce went to feed the Japanese army. We actually were allowed to keep very little of what we grew.

Pig weed had taken over the farm and we were kept busy trying to get rid of it. The weed is a nuisance and grows wild in the Philippines, and it has little or no food value. However, if guards were agreeable, we carried armloads of the stuff into the camp where we boiled it in tin cans at the quan stove. We ate until we were bloated.

Contrary to what one might think, the farm was not a pleasant place to work. We were constantly surrounded by stern guards, one of whom was always the overseer. Overseers were picked for their meanness. Farm guards were exceptionally cruel and gave orders which were always accompanied by kicks and blows from pickax handles. Without except, when they shouted out an order, a kick followed. It was expected.

It didn't take long for us to choose appropriate

names for each guard. Donald Duck was a neurotic with a bad temper, just like the cartoon character when things didn't go his way. He would rave and rant at us in Japanese and vent his frustrations by running up and down our line striking mercilessly whoever was nearest with a shovel or anything that was within reach. He even sounded just like Donald Duck.

Then there was Charlie Chaplin. His behavior toward us was similar to Donald Duck's except that his actions were not accompanied by raving or ranting. Charlie's beatings were given in silence, just as Chaplin had performed in the silent movies. Except Chaplin's antics were funny; his were not.

One of the Seven Dwarfs from Snow White was also represented. He was Smiley. He appeared to be in good-humored all the time, with a happy, pleasant smile on his face. Only it wasn't a smile! It was his natural expression that served to cover up his mean disposition. His favorite way of venting his frustrations was to find any excuse he could to beat someone with a pickax handle. He loved to beat up prisoners for the fun of it. There were many instances when we had to carry men back to the barracks on stretchers after he had worked them over. His superiors did nothing to stop him. They thought it was humorous.

One afternoon I was caught haplessly in Donald Duck's wrath. We were planting cabbages under his supervision and as we were bent over, putting the small plants into the ground, Donald came running toward me yelling and screaming at the top of his lungs. I knew for some unknown reason I was in trouble and quickly came to attention. Lucky for me there were no farm tools within his reach. He came up and struck me with both his fists, knocking me to the ground. I bounced up, and again he knocked me to the ground. Somehow, with all the effort I could muster, I continued to get back on my feet after every blow. He must have been hurting himself for he finally gave up in disgust and walked away. It was then I noticed a guard had been standing by with a fixed bayonet, waiting for me to do something. Fortunately I hadn't. That night I had a difficult time sleeping with my bruised and battered body.

One man who knew Japanese better than most of us came up to me that night as I laid in pain and explained that Donald Duck had complained that I was planting the cabbages one inch too deep in the holes. "Be more careful next time," he said. His words weren't much of a comfort.

Fertilizing the fields on the farm was not very popular among the men, for obvious reasons. We were ordered to dip the human excreta out of the latrines and load it into fifty-gallon gas drums. Each drum was then suspended on two poles which four men carried out to the farm where the contents were scattered over the fields. Most of us had no shoes so it was necessary to walk barefoot over the newly fertilized ground. The smell from the fields was abominable. As the result of fertilizing with human waste, everything grown on the farm had to be cooked before it could be eaten. No farm worker ever dared eat raw vegetables.

When we first came to the prison camp at Cabanatuan, water had been scarce. As storage was increased, our water supply became more and more adequate and we could even shower regularly. However, not all the men bathed for various reasons. Some were too weak to even attempt it, while others had lost their spirit and didn't care whether they were clean or not. Dirt and filth didn't seem to bother them.

Some of us were proud possessors of five-gallon cans which we cherished dearly. We warmed our bath water by filling our cans in the morning and putting them where they would be exposed to the hot sun all day. By late afternoon, when we came back from the farm, the water was warm and soothing to our dirty bodies.

We learned to organize our baths efficiently to make the best use of the warm water. It became a precise ritual. Using a canteen cup as a dipper, a bather would slowly pour the first cup over his head and let the water run down his body. The next cup he would pour over the left shoulder with the left arm stiffened against the body. The third cup was poured over the right shoulder with the right arm stiff against the body. There was a cup of water for the chest, one for the back, and then one for the right and one for the left hip. Once we were wet, we rubbed our body vigorously. Then we rinsed off our bodies with the same procedure, starting with the head, ending with the hips. We did all this without soap. The vigorous rubbing got much of the dirt from our bodies. And it certainly made us feel much better. We looked forward to our evening baths.

As the months passed, we learned ways to improve our diet. For instance, we began getting carabao soup once a week. We were rationed one carabao for the camp, for 50,000 men. We learned, however, that when the animal was slaughtered, the blood was discarded. What a waste! We then come up with the bright idea that the blood could be used. The next time a carabao was slaughtered, we collected the blood in our trusty five-gallon cans and then boiled it on the quan until it coagulated. We had no spices, nothing to mix with it, but we found when we spread it over our rice, it helped kill the sickening mildew flavor. And there's no doubt, it had to be somewhat nourishing. After that first experiment, not one drop of the carabao blood was wasted.

Another important breakthrough for us was the development of hominy from corn. The little corn that we received for our labor was of such poor quality, and so hard to digest, that it usually gave us the runs. One prisoner from Alabama remembered his mother making hominy. He did his best to recall how she did it. The results weren't the best southern hominy grits in the world, but it did improve the taste. And after we learned to make hominy, our diet improved tremendously. We no longer minded that the Japanese took the better grade of corn. Food value wise it made no difference.

They say that necessity is the mother of invention. Nowhere did it apply better than in prison camp. We threw nothing away, not even the corncobs after we removed the corn. The Japanese allowance of three or four squares of toilet paper per week was far from adequate, especially for a man suffering from dysentery. The corncobs, although rough and uncomfortable, supplemented the rationed toilet paper.

There was a secret black market operating in camp between prisoners with money and Japanese guards. Money was exchanged mainly for rice and other foodstuffs. One man I knew had made a deal with a Japanese guard who periodically dumped a sack of rice over the fence. The man then hid the rice in a container concealed within a table with a false bottom. The table at a glance appeared to be like all the other rustic tables around camp. It was an ingenuous contraption that took much skill to construct. The top was hinged and when it was raised there was the rice, sometimes a couple of kilos. So cleverly was it fashioned that the Japanese inspection parties that walked past noticed nothing unusual. The risk this man took was considerable but the rice he obtained—which was the same rice the Japanese kept for themselves—was clean, free of grubs and far superior to the rice they gave us.

Those who had money could purchase a canteen cup of rice from the owner. Most of the money went back to the Japanese supplier.

In time we also discovered that making rice flour was a simple matter. We soaked the rice in the water and then dried it in the sun. Once rice is dry, it becomes soft, and we could then roll it with a bottle to make flour. By mixing rice flour again with water, we could make hotcake batter which we cooked on the quan stove. No Log Cabin syrup, of course.

Sometime in 1943, the Japanese command began paying us for working on the farm. Our salary was about six centavos a month. After we began receiving pay for our work, the Japanese allowed a truck every now and then to enter the camp loaded with coconuts and bananas, and a little tobacco. Most of us could only afford to purchase a coconut or a banana or two but the opportunity to buy something extra was perhaps more psychologically beneficial than the little nourishment we received from whatever we bought.

Among prisoners' most valuable possessions were empty sterile bandage cans. We called them our "butt cans," and in these small containers each of us stored every shred of discarded cigarettes that we could find. Generally, every cigarette was totally smoked, down to the last grain of tobacco, making it almost impossible to find butts anywhere on the ground. But occasionally someone did toss away some remnants of a butt, especially passing Japanese officers, and these we searched for constantly. We walked around with our eyes glued to the ground. To get the most from the tobacco I found, I made a rough looking pipe from local hardwood. I smoked it occasionally, very occasionally, for tobacco was scarce and expensive to buy, even from friends.

Then came my sensational discovery!

It happened that the Japanese decided to let our officers play softball once a week in an adjoining field not used by the prisoners. One day, while talking to some friends and watching the softball game out of the corner of my eye, I noticed that several ball players were smoking as they played. I immediately thought about the butts. I gradually moved away from my friends, and at the same time continued to watch the game. A batter took a swing and sent the ball flying to the outfield where an outfielder, seeing it coming, flipped his almost whole cigarette to the ground and ran to catch the ball. I couldn't believe it! I had discovered an area untouched by cigarette butt hunters.

The next day I did not work on the farm, and when the chance came, I casually strolled over to the playing field, by myself, and conducted a thorough search. There were no cigarette butts at home plate since the batter and catcher had been too busy to smoke, but behind the plate there were several butts. I went to check each base in the infield, and sure enough there were a few butts at each base. But it was the outfield that proved to be a bonanza. There were cigarette butts scattered everywhere.

I went back to the barracks with my butt can overflowing and one pocket almost filled. I made up my mind to keep my discovery a secret. For reasons no one could understand, I suddenly became vitally interested ball games, nor could anyone understand why my butt can was never empty. I now had plenty of pipe tobacco.

Cabanatuan was located in the middle of a plain. The land was flat and extended as far as the eye could see. During the rainy season, violent storms struck our area with wind velocities of well over sixty miles per hour. As storms approached, we could look out across the plain and see a solid black wall of rain clouds rapidly advancing toward us.

If we were outside, we barely had enough time to snatch our belongings and make it to the barracks. The barracks were open on both ends and without doors or windows. An open space under our sleeping areas created an ideal wind tunnel. Gusts of wind accompanied by heavy rain tore through the building from end to end leaving everything soaked in its path. Lightning flashed and the thunder boomed like cannons. There is nothing that will equal a thunder storm in the tropics.

One night during such a violent storm, a prisoner got up and went to the doorway to view the lightning. I could see him standing there, the flashes of lightening silhouetting him in the door frame. Suddenly a bolt of lightening struck the doorway, and the man was electrocuted as he stood there. The next morning everyone went to silently examine the charred and burned doorway. Even Mother Nature was working against us.

We had a special area set aside in Cabanatuan that was really deplorable, but at the same time necessary. It was for unstable and insecure soldiers, those who might become violent or take their own lives. These men were stripped of all their clothes and kept in a guarded enclosed area in full view of everyone. Three or four times a day they were led to the latrines, tied together with ropes around their waists, like dogs on a leash. Their antics were often abnormal and there was always the fear that they might commit suicide.

On one occasion, a man came to me and blurted out that he didn't see why anyone should have to live under these conditions. As he spoke, he placed his forearm before my eyes and I observed a cut exposing an artery on his wrist. He was at the end of his line. To save his life I had no choice other than to recommend that he be put with the others. Another man in my barracks frequently fell into spells of laughter for no reason. He too had to be led away to join the unstable group.

One prisoner in my barracks had a Latin sounding

name and when I questioned him about it, he told me he was Italian. He had been on Corregidor during the siege, and one day, after I befriended him, he waved me into a corner, and looking around suspiciously, said, "You must swear you will tell no one." Not knowing what else to say, I agreed. He then told me a tale that sent shivers up my spine.

It appeared that just before the surrender, an officer had commanded him to help bury a burlap sack, which, in due course, he discovered contained two heavy bars of gold. He surmised that the officer was killed and only he knew where the gold was buried. After the war he was going to be a very rich man. I had no idea why he was telling me this, unless he wished me to have the gold if something happened to him. Whatever it was, he was very disturbed and as a result had trouble sleeping at night. Day and night he planned how he would recover the gold. He never left the barracks; he just sat there and brooded about his secret.

One day when I returned from the farm my Italian friend was gone. I inquired what had happened to him, only to learn that he had been taken away. My first thought was that the Japanese had somehow discovered his secret. I then learned he had been relocated; he had been placed with the other misfits. He had never been on Corregidor as he claimed.

I had gained some experience in the physiotherapy clinic during my short stay at Sternberg General Hospital while in Manila. Based on this brief experience, I was now assigned to cover the wards and manipulate the arms and legs of patients who were bedridden. I walked around with a bottle of mineral oil from one bed to another. This work, the physical contact, the helping of others, the exercise, had much to do with my own well-being and perhaps even my own survival.

Through my work in the hospital I met endless people, each with his own problem. Some had strange things happen to them. There was a Navy chief who had contracted syphilis just before the surrender. The disease was in an advanced stage and had paralyzed his legs and affected his vocal chords. We had no medicine and there was nothing we could do for him, except comfort him. He spoke only two words, and these he used vociferously whenever he became frustrated or angry. They were "goddam" and "sonofabitch."

The chief was a real career Navy man, with tattoos all over his body. Across his back was tattooed a dragon that extended from his shoulders to his waist. On his chest was a big cross with clouds in the background. His arms and legs were marked with various signs and figures.

When we first started to work with the chief, he was bed ridden and could only move his arms. With our help, he improved rapidly and soon we had him in a sitting position. His attitude was good and he had a great deal of courage. He made desperate attempts to walk, but he always fell over, and when he did the whole ward heard him as he called out, "Goddam, sonofabitch."

Through his persistence we had him walking within a few weeks, but he could not manipulate his left leg. He stepped with his right and dragged his left. We made a cane for him and he was doing very well. I lost track of him not long after that. It was so strange, how someone could be around one minute and the next they were gone, and you never knew what happened to them.

Chapter 18

CHANGING THE GUARD

Life continued, but barely, in Camp Cabanatuan. It would be difficult to say if things got better or worse; we only knew that to preserve life we had to learn to tolerate conditions as they were. We did the best we could with what we had, and we waited. Even time lost its meaning. A week was the same as a month. Months became years. They all blended into one impression.

We learned from necessity to make what clothing we needed. We fashioned wooden shoes from 2x4s and leather straps. We had no razors so shaving was impossible; but we did have barbers and everyone kept his hair short and trimmed. Our skin from the tropical sun had turned dark, the color of mahogany.

The Japanese command did permit us to have our own entertainment once a week. We organized a band. I have no idea where the musical instruments for our band came from, but we did somehow manage to put together a five-piece band that we considered outstanding. We were very proud of our band.

Aside from band music we acted out short skits. Some of these theatrical performances depicted various situations in camp that were intended to be funny, and others depicted personalities. We could at least laugh at ourselves. Some skits portrayed life back in the States.

There was a black man who brought down the house one night. He was from an artillery outfit, and the only black prisoner of war I had seen in camp. That night he danced what he called "Beriberi Shuffle" and imitated the men who had sore feet. His imitation was so close to reality that we laughed until we were almost sick.

Occasionally the Japanese had their own special brand of entertainment for their soldiers which we would watch from a distance. They like to hold contests, both group and individual contests. Some of their games were more funny than our skits, although it wasn't intended to be that way. We were highly amused as we watched them play the kids' game "Drop the Handkerchief." We used to play the same game in primary grades. This always brought snickers from the prisoners and it was all we could do to keep from bursting out laughing. Here was our enemy, running around in circles dropping handkerchiefs. But we dared not laugh aloud. The Japanese took their games very seriously.

Early in 1943, the Japanese command decided to replace the Cabanatuan guards with new Japanese recruits from Formosa. We guessed the move was to provide more troops for the battle fields. Perhaps the war was going badly for the Japanese, but it was only a guess.

Camp Cabanatuan by this time had been divided into two areas, one designated as the hospital and other as the duty or farm area. Between these two areas was a grassy open field which the Japanese used to train these new recruits. The training sessions often reminded me of the Mack Sennett comedies, popular during the twenties. The poor recruits, their biggest difficulty was mastering the Japanese rifle. The Japanese rifle was of very poor quality and the bolt often stuck. It was amusing to watch as the sergeant-in-charge shouted the command for the recruits to slide open the bolts, followed by an immediate command to snap them shut. Almost without fail, at least one or two soldiers would be left struggling to snap the bolts shut, without success. This failure to close the bolts always angered the sergeant-in-charge. He would then walk up to the recruit, slap him across the face and sometimes kick him at the same time. The recruit would hastily try to correct his error. If he was unable to shut the bolt, amid more blows and screams, the sergeant would snatch the rifle away and attempt to demonstrate the correct procedure for handling a rifle inspection. But sometimes the sergeant-in-charge couldn't close the bolt either, and if he too failed, he would go in to a rage. We were always amused by these maneuvers and we were hardly able to contain our laughter, at least until we got back to the barracks. Then we would crack up. We knew what the consequences would be if we laughed at Japanese soldiers in their presence.

Another time Japanese recruits were going through a training exercise that involved simulating an attack on a machine gun position, which, in this case, was located on an anthill at the top of the training field. The sergeant-in-charge wielded a big club as he ran about shouting out orders. There were about forty men in this group, lying on the ground pretending to fire their guns at the imaginary enemy. The sergeant gave the order for the left flank to advance about fifty paces. He then ordered the right flank to move up, and finally the men in the center. The maneuver was repeated several times until the sergeant seemed satisfied. They were now ready to make the final charge at the anthill on top the hill. The sergeant's command rang out to fix bayonets, whereby his men reached around to their scabbards, withdrew their bayonets and locked them in place on their rifles. All except one man. This poor unfortunate fellow's bayonet would not snap into place. The sergeant-in-charge saw that the soldier was having trouble and went charging at him across the field, waving his club over his head as he ran.

At this moment someone gave the order to charge. The whole group, including the man in trouble, began charging toward the anthill, shouting "banzai!" As they ran up the hill, it was apparent the unfortunate recruit knew the sergeant with the club was close behind him. Wild-eyed, he put on a burst of speed and disappeared over the top of the anthill, still struggling with his bayonet. We could only guess at what happened when the sergeant met up with the recruit on the other side of the mound.

All prisoners, regardless who we were, officer or enlisted man, were required to either salute or bow as we passed a Japanese soldier in camp. Nor were we permitted to keep our hands in our pockets. We learned to live with this ritual, although, as prisoners of war, we had become pretty informal about differences within our own ranks. The Japanese, on the other hand, considered it military courtesy and demanded respect, even among themselves.

There was one guard post on the main road that led through the middle of camp where we had to be especially careful. We used this road only occasionally, but when we passed the post, we made sure that we came to attention and either bowed or saluted the guards.

I was standing near the post one day when I saw a prisoner coming down the road. He walked past the post without bowing or saluting. Although there was nothing in his appearance that distinguished him from any other prisoner, I recognized him at once as one of our chaplains. I knew he was in for serious trouble. A guard immediately jumped down, ran up to the chaplain and slapped him in the face. He didn't stop there. He delivered a dozen more blows, finally knocking the chaplain down and began kicking him. While the chaplain lay in the dust in agony, the guard returned to his station.

I talked to the chaplain after the incident. I explained that Japanese military courtesy required that a prisoner regardless of whom he might be must turn toward the guard post and salute, and that he must not have a hand in his pocket. The chaplain had been guilty of these two infractions of their rules. He didn't admit it but I had the feeling that as a chaplain he felt he was beyond such regulations. The Japanese thought differently.

That night after the incident, as I lay on the floor in the barracks trying to fall asleep, I thought how easily it would have been for the guard to bayonet or even shoot the chaplain. He could easily have done so.

Maybe it was the thought of the guard using his gun that prompted my mind to wander to another incident involving a gun. I was a young boy in San Francisco.

In my mind I could see so clearly the three flats in our building, each crowded with people, and each containing a Machi family. In our family, counting our grandfather Nonno and grandmother Nonna, my mother and father and all my brothers and sisters, there were twelve of us who lived on the lower floor. Then Aunt Mary, Uncle Tom and their six children lived in the middle flat. On the top floor lived Aunt Rose and Uncle Mike and their four children. Years may have passed but I could see them all so clearly, twenty-six Machis in our three families. I could even count them—two grandparents, six parents, and eighteen children!

Squabbles among the children and among the adult members were a daily occurrence, due, no doubt, to our crowded conditions. But as serious as arguments may have seemed at the time were quickly forgotten. The one that stuck out most vividly in my mind, however, nearly had serious consequences.

It happened one day when I was returning home from school. I came around the corner and was surprised to see a small crowd gathered in front of our house. I edged my way through the crowd to where I could see what was happening. At first it appeared to be just another family squabble. Hanging out the windows upstairs were Mama, Aunt Mary, Aunt Rose and some older children. They were jabbering and shouting all at once, waving their arms and pointing fingers in all directions. It was difficult to tell what was happening, but it was obvious that the spectators on the sidewalk had already chosen sides. Some were shouting back while others encouraged them on.

Suddenly Uncle Mike burst out of his flat and appeared on the landing in front, waving a six-shooter. Spectators instantly ducked for cover and windows slammed shut. I couldn't for the world imagine who Uncle Mike was going to shoot, but I did know this was really serious.

Now it was the women's turn to act. Mama, Aunt Mary and Aunt Rose appeared in the next instant and struggled with Uncle Mike on the staircase until they took the gun away from him. They led him upstairs, spectators came out of hiding and peace reigned again on our street. It was just another day in the Machi family.

Besides working on the farm I was assigned to assist in the medical laboratory when needed. Amoebic dysentery was playing havoc with the prisoners, and also affecting the Japanese. Our American doctors convinced the Japanese authorities that we had to isolate those with amoebic dysentery. The doctors were granted their request that a separate area be set aside for such prisoners. We established a makeshift laboratory for the purpose of collecting and studying our stool specimens. As long as the dysentery bug was dormant, it did not create a problem. It was during its active stages that it became dangerous, and it was better to place the men in isolation than to take chances on the disease spreading.

Being close to the disease, we who worked in the lab had to be periodically checked, and one morning I discovered my stool was contaminated. I was ordered to pack my belongings and move to the amoebic dysentery area. My isolation, however, did not exclude me from working on the farm. I was in the farm crew lineup every morning.

Chapter 19

THE BLACK MARKET
DEATH SENTENCE

In spite of severe punishment meted out by the Japanese to prisoners involved in black market activities, there were those who would not give up. They not only bought and sold items to other prisoners but they were also brazen enough to sell to the Japanese.

While I was in isolation with dysentery, I was able to watch the black market action take place within the camp. I could easily understand the motives of those who dealt in the black market. Prisoners had a difficult time improving their conditions in camp, but dealing in the market was one way out. If others could do it, why couldn't I? After reassuring myself that I was just as bright as any of those involved, and that my standard of living could be better, I decided to take the chance and go into business.

I borrowed ten pesos from a friend, five of which was spent to buy empty corned beef cans. My next move was to visit the black marketeer in rice. Seeing that I had five pesos to spend, he lifted the false top on his table and sold me a canteen cup of rice. I then rolled the rice into flour, borrowed some sourdough starter, added water to the starter and allowed it to set overnight. Early the next morning, I put the batter in my corned beef cans and baked it in the quan stove oven.

I doubt that even a hungry, starving dog in the alleys back home would have eaten my biscuits, but they tasted good to me and they were easy to sell.

I had limited my efforts to the amoebic dysentery area the first day, but business was so brisk I decided to expand into the duty area. I had a friend in the duty area and we decided to become partners. We conducted business matters while talking through the barbed wire fence that separated the duty from the dysentery area. I would be responsible for keeping the tins and money while my partner would bake the biscuits in the quan stove and sell them in his area. We would split the profits equally.

Meanwhile, a detail of American prisoners was sent to a warehouse in town every morning to pick up the day's ration of rice that had come from Manila for the whole camp. It was in these rice sacks that friends of the black market profiteers were smuggling Japanese paper money into our area of the camp. All would have gone well except that a couple of profiteers had unwisely begun to use this money to buy items from the truck that visited the camp once a week.

The Japanese became suspicious when they discovered that the amount of money they were receiving from the truck sales far exceeded the amount they paid us for farm work. Secretly they investigated and uncovered the smuggling ring. Patiently they awaited their moment to strike. How lucky can one get. At dawn the day before my partner and I were to expand the biscuit business, a squad of enemy soldiers rushed through the main gate and ran to designated locations around the duty area. They grabbed about twenty alleged profiteers and marched them away. We never saw them again, nor did we ever hear what happened to them. We assumed they were beheaded as this was the penalty for black marketeers. I immediately lost interest in the biscuit business and that was the last time I entertained thoughts of carrying on an illegal business in prison.

U.S. Prisoners of war in camp.

Chapter 20

FOOD RELIEF
THAT NEVER CAME

———◂◆▸———

Filipino agencies repeatedly attempted to bring food to our camp but were unsuccessful. We frequently saw trucks loaded with supplies turned away from our gates. No Red Cross or international representatives were allowed to enter the camp. We figured the Japanese did not want to be embarrassed by their inability to account for the condition of the prisoners and the many thousands of people who had died of disease and starvation. This attitude continued until shortly before Christmas, 1943, when they allowed the first Red Cross food packages into camp.

This was our first sign of hope. One cannot adequately describe the impact it had on our lives. The boxes contained cans of corned beef and cheese, bars of chocolate, packages of dried fruits, packs of vitamins— everything we needed so badly and which we had been without for so long. We didn't immediately tear everything open as one might suspect, but instead we held the items in our hands, turning them over and over, tears streaming down our cheeks.

Aside from food and vitamins, some boxes contained much needed hospital and medical supplies. Packed in Red Cross boxes were Atabrine, quinine and sulfa drugs. We now had the tools to help fight tropical diseases. Within a few weeks we could see the difference; the death toll was reduced dramatically, almost over night.

We carefully rationed the food and placed a supply of drugs on shelves in each building. One morning we found three men lying unconscious on the ground outside their barracks. They had taken a drug overdose. For three days they were left to lay there, and almost everyone in camp filed by to take a look. The drugs were quickly removed from the buildings and placed in the hospital ward under guard.

A few months after the arrival of the Red Cross packages we received our first packages from home. Prisoners cried openly as they opened boxes addressed to them. Our first thoughts were that our families must have known all along that we were still alive. Most of us tried to find places where we could be alone with our boxes, knowing that they had been packed by members of our family or by our girl friends.

For those few brief moments it were as though our families and loved ones were with us. I found a secluded spot and slowly opened my box. I had to smile, for obviously my family wanted me to be the best dressed man in camp. They hadn't realized that my greatest need was for food. Inside the box, neatly folded, was a pair of pants, a shirt, some underwear, a tooth brush, a tube of toothpaste and a container of vitamins, but no food.

Naturally, men who worked in the kitchen had more access to food, so I asked for and got a job on the breakfast shift. Our crew had to get up at two o'clock in the morning to start the fires and boil the rice. We stirred the rice with large paddles until it became a soupy mixture which we called lugao, the Filipino name for porridge. It was moldy in taste and loaded with weevils and grubs. After the lugao was served early each morning, I usually went back to the barracks and tried to get some sleep.

Sometimes instead of sleeping I tried to picture Shelter Cove. The best thoughts were of those summers with the old gang in which we had such fun. I relived those moments over and over.

Many stockholders in the San Francisco International Fish company sent their sons to help with the fishing during the summer. The Italians were well represented, and like the permanent staff at the cove I could remember every one of their names laying in my bunk—Peter Tarantino, Frank and Peter Alioto, Tom and Frank Balestrieri, Andrew Machi, and my brother Babe. All us were about the same age. As the summer wore on, we developed a playful competition between us boys and the adults. The adults were just as mischievous as the boys, if not worse. They slipped garter snakes into our beds, and we threw eggs at them and put burlap sacks in their chimneys to make them smoke. It was all in good fun with each trying to outdo the other's pranks. The furthest thought from our minds was war in the Pacific.

At the end of that season, as we were getting ready to go back to school, a crowd gathered on the dock to say farewell to us. We felt so proud as we began to board the boat, and then the eggs started to fly. The crew who were still on shore had decided to give us an egg bath as we boarded. Not to be outdone, the captain ran into the galley and gathered up all his eggs and began flinging them at the crew on shore. The battle didn't stop until the boat pulled away from the dock.

I remembered how sad it was when the season came to an end. Departing fishing boats each gave three blasts of their whistles, meaning "Good-bye," "Good Luck" and "God Bless You." What happy memories: days of growing up, working, and enjoying the company good friends. I longed for those days again; I longed for Shelter Cove; I felt that no other place in the world could provide as beautiful a setting and atmosphere for a group of city boys as Shelter Cove. Certainly Cabanatuan could not. Such wonderful thoughts were all I needed.

I was having these pleasant thoughts one morning

when I went to my bunk after finishing kitchen duty and laid down. I don't remember the exact day it was, but I do remember the month and the year. Until my dying day I shall never forget that moment.

Chapter 21

BOMBERS IN THE SKY

———◆——

The struggle to recapture the Philippines, vital to General MacArthur's war plans, began on the morning of October 20,1944, when four divisions of the U.S. Sixth Army under Lt. Gen. Walter Krueger landed on Leyte's east coast between Tacloban and Dulag. General Douglas MacArthur was with them and went ashore with the first landing party, thus fulfilling his pledge to return...HS

It must have been about ten o'clock in the morning when I was aroused by a roaring noise in the sky. For a moment I thought I was back in Shelter Cove, and the roaring was the sound of engines of fishing boats leaving the harbor. But when I opened my eyes I wasn't in Shelter Cove; I was still in Camp Cabanatuan.

The roar grew louder. Fully awake now, I jumped out of my bunk and dashed outside as fast as I could. Standing there in front of the all the barracks were the prisoners, looking up at the sky. I squinted against the sharp glare of the morning light, and there, flying in tight formation, was a squadron of about a hundred dive bombers with fighter planes circling counterclockwise around them. They appeared to be headed toward Clark Airfield. It was impossible to see what insignias they carried on their wings, but we surmised they were U.S. aircraft. One thing certain, they were not Japanese.

As soon as the planes had passed over and beyond the camp, the rumors started buzzing. Every man, down to those who were even too weak to leave their bunks, talked excitedly about the appearance of the planes, but everyone did so with restraint. Without anyone telling us, we knew we had to show self-control. We were aware that anyone who demonstrated emotion over the arrival of the planes would be dealt with severely by the Japanese. We had to keep mum. But how difficult that was to do.

Some prisoners believed the planes might be English; others thought they were American; while there were those who weren't sure what they were. "If they are not British and not American, then who are they?" the skeptics asked.. The arguments started. The arguments were finally settled when a half hour later another flight of a hundred or more planes came into view and flew over the camp. This time there was no question about them. We could plainly see the stars. They were American planes.

It took all the effort we had to restrain our excitement now. We had questions; we wanted to make remarks; but we continued to play mum. We all wanted to jump, shout for joy, go crazy, but the fear of retaliation by the Japanese held us back. Some men simply smiled through their tears. We didn't need words. I was weak with emotion, and ever so proud of my country. No one will ever know what the sight of those planes meant to us. Those poor thousands of prisoners who died, who were starved, who were tortured to death, if they could only have held out. Strange, but now I felt my deepest compassion for them, now when they could have been saved. Thank the lord I helped many stay alive for this moment.

Two days later the guards lined us up in the open area of the camp. We had no idea what they intended to do at this point. It was not beyond them to execute us as a final gesture to the emperor. Or perhaps they planned to hold us as hostages, as a bargaining chip for later.

As guards were holding roll call and counting us, another flight of planes flew over the camp, but this time at a much higher altitude. We were now fearful that at the height they were flying the American pilots might think we were Japanese and drop down to strafe us. But they didn't, and we were contented now that they knew where our prison camp was located. Help was sure to arrive.

But no one came to rescue us. Instead Japanese headquarters issued orders that we were to be moved to Bilibid Prison in Manila and, from there, placed on a transport for Japan. We were right after all. They were going to hold us as hostages.

Guards with fixed bayonets jammed us into trucks and, after traveling all day, we arrived at the prison. We had left behind over 1,800 men in the graveyard at Camp Cabanatuan.

Chapter 22

FROM CABANATUAN
TO BILIBID PRISON

————◆◆◆————

Manila's Bilibid had been a civilian prison long before the Japanese invaded the islands. A high concrete wall surrounded the old prison, and the buildings inside were arranged around a square. A few of the buildings had been used as sleeping quarters for the guards, while others provided work places for the prisoners. There were windows but no glass remained; the openings had been nailed shut with boards.

In the middle of the prison was an outdoor courtyard. On one side was a two-story building that appeared to have been used for administration. Guards herded us into the courtyard and assigned us to our quarters. A few prisoners were assigned to individual bunks. I was a lucky one.

A number of U.S. Navy men had been interned in Bilibid since their capture three years before and were still there when we arrived. Many of these seamen were in the Philippines before the war and had experience in dealing with Asians. We called them old Asian hands. I met one chief petty officer who, I was told, knew the ropes and had outwitted many a Japanese soldier. He was a corpsman and he often treated men who had contracted venereal disease.

VD was not a real problem in the American army if treated properly. If a soldier contracted the disease, he was sent to the hospital where he received treatment and was then released. He was not necessarily chastised. By contrast, if a Japanese soldier was caught with the infection, he was beaten unmercifully before he was treated. As a result, Japanese soldiers at Bilibid tried to treat themselves before they were caught. Sulfathiazole was in great demand for the treatment of gonorrhea. The drug came in the form of pills with the letter "W" engraved on each tablet indicating that the manufacturer was the Winthrop Drug Company. The navy chief had become quite proficient in inscribing fake pills with whatever letters were desired. The fake VD pills were made from plaster of Paris and were inscribed with the letter "W". These were sold to the Japanese who wanted to treat themselves rather than take a beating. The chief and his cronies developed a thriving business, trading their plaster of Paris for privileges and sacks of rice and sugar.

As we stood by waiting for a boat to transfer us to Japan, U.S. Air Force dive bombers pounded the waterfront day after day. From inside the prison we watched the air raids as planes flew above the city, and we could see the anti-aircraft barrages sent up by the Japanese. Frequently we caught glimpses of air battles between American and Japanese fighter planes.

I was working in the kitchen one day when a dogfight took place directly over our heads. We could see that one plane was hit; smoke poured from its fuselage as it began to spin and fall toward earth. We held our breaths. We couldn't tell if it were American or Japanese. As it neared the ground, the insignia of the Rising Sun became visible to everyone, including the guards. They saw us looking at the falling plane and immediately began hitting us as if we were to blame for what happened. It was one beating we didn't mind.

The day for our transfer to Japan finally came. A troop ship was brought in under the cover of darkness and waited in the harbor. Both Japanese and American administrative officers and men worked the night through compiling lists of those who would leave. Mostly officers were on the transfer roster, and that included just about every officer in our company. Some 250 men who were too weak to be moved were to be left behind with a skeleton crew of medics to take care of them. I was one of those chosen to remain behind. I was dumbfounded. Why me, I protested, but to no avail. I desperately wanted to go with the rest of the prisoners.

The next morning the officers and men lined up to leave, and I rushed among them, shaking the hands of my friends and wishing them good luck. They looked somber, knowing that American planes flew overhead daily. Many felt that they would never reach Japan. It was a premonition they had.

Just as the men were about to be marched out the gate, guards came down the line, recognized one of the prisoners and pulled him from the line. "He is Swiss," I heard someone say. The Japanese were acknowledging that Swiss nationals were not involved in the war. It took them three years to find out.

I watched the prisoners leave, nearly 1,800 men, many who were my friends. We had come this far together and now they were gone. I then went back behind the walls to attend to the sick. I had to keep busy.

The next day the tragic news reached us in prison that the ship carrying our men had been sunk by American planes; there were few survivors. This we found hard to believe. We knew that according to international law, a ship carrying prisoners of war in a battle zone was to be clearly marked as a neutral ship. It was reported that the Japanese had failed to mark the vessel as a prisoner of war ship. The Japanese confirmed the fact a few days later. I was sick at heart at the loss of so many of my friends. They had survived more than three years of misery, starvation and torture only to die when victory was so close at hand.

The 250 men left behind in Bilibid were starving and in very bad condition. As ill as they were, their survival depended upon finding whatever food they could to eat. They looked so pathetic scavenging for things to eat. A few men found the location where the kitchen staff threw out their garbage, and here they rummaged for scraps. These dreadfully sick men would sit in the middle of the garbage heap, garbage that stunk from rot and decay, and turn over every scrap, stuffing into their mouths everything and anything that appeared to be edible. We knew that much of the garbage was contaminated, but there was little we could do to get the men to stop eating it.

One man, because of the coloration of his skin, stood out from all the others. He was very pale and ashen, like a telephone book, and he would not listen to anyone who tried to discourage him from eating garbage. After a few days I saw them carry his body to the graveyard, a victim of food poisoning as well as malnutrition.

After the man's death, a memorandum was sent to all ward surgeons and building leaders instructing them that patients had been seen eating garbage that had been designated for the pigs, and that the garbage could cause a fatal type of food poisoning. The memorandum further stated that all personnel were forbidden from handling as well as eating garbage at any time. What the memorandum didn't say was that starving men don't always hear. Many continued to sit on the garbage heap and eat poisoned food

To discourage anyone from trying to escape from Bilibid, a high-powered electrical wire had been placed on the top of the high concrete wall that surrounded the prison. At one point the wall ran close to Japanese headquarters where some soldiers lived. Windows with steel bars faced the wall. One night we were awakened to a loud scream, and the next morning we learned the cause. Apparently during the night a Japanese soldier had to urinate and rather than go downstairs to the latrine he decided to relieve himself out the window. As his urine touched the wire, it conducted electricity to his body, killing him instantly. He never knew what hit him. He may have been our enemy but for once we couldn't help feeling a strange sort of pity. What a way to die!

American planes continued to bomb the waterfront daily. We were thrilled and excited whenever our planes appeared. We spent hours in the open courtyard turning over rumors about how the war was going, and, of course, trying to figure out what the Japanese would eventually do with us. We even considered that the end might come when an American bomb landed in the prison.

One night we were awakened by the sound of trucks entering the compound. They did not sound like Japanese vehicles. We then heard loud voices and a much shouting. The voices were not all Japanese. We heard American voices, men's voices, and then, unbelievably, we heard American women and the voices of children. These were the first voices of women and children we had heard in three years! We couldn't sleep the rest of the night, wondering what was going on.

The next morning we learned the voices were those of civilian prisoners who had been brought in from a camp nearby and were now being housed in the two-story administration building. Then we saw them, women and children, standing on the steps. Although we were forbidden to go near them, it didn't take us long to get communications started.

One of our men found a piece of board and scribbled a message on it with a hunk of plaster. He held it up so that the new inmates could read it. Our communication system was crude but it worked. While messages were being exchanged, men were positioned around the prison to alert us if guards were in the vicinity.

Information about loved ones who had not seen each other for three years was passed back and forth for several days.

During our stay at Cabanatuan, the Japanese had steadfastly refused our medical staff permission to perform autopsies on our dead soldiers.

At Bilibid, however, they finally relented. Shortly after permission was granted, I was assigned as the clean-up man in the autopsy room. Several autopsies involving amoebic dysentery were performed exposing perforated intestines. On one occasion, shortly after the body of a prisoner had been opened and examined, the remains were placed in a sack for burial. As the Japanese detail came to bury him, the soldier in charge, to my amazement, commanded the other soldiers to come to attention. They then saluted the dead man. I knew at that moment that something was up. This was totally out of character for Japanese soldiers. And I had been right. We learned that same day that the American army had landed at Lingayen Gulf and was on its way to Manila. Obviously, the Japanese soldier in charge of the burial detail was suddenly concerned about his own future. Not all Japanese soldiers were prepared to die for their emperor.

Rumors were flying everywhere and we were certain an invasion was imminent, but when, and where? We didn't know what to expect. All we could do was listen to the rumors, and wait.

One evening just before dark, we were in the courtyard when we were startled by the roar of motor vehicles. A machine gun opened fire and guns from the street returned fire. Although we were protected by a high concrete wall, we still ran for cover. We were unable to determine what was what was going on, but the firing continued all night long.

We had very little sleep that night and everyone was

up early the next morning, and greatly excited. We could see from the cracks between the boards in our windows that American tanks had surrounded the prison during the night and were continuing to press the battle that morning.

*Food and medical supplies being dropped
to the Allied internees at Bilibid Prison.*

Chapter 23

RESCUE FROM BILIBID

———◆◆◆———

The Japanese commander, Gen. Tomoyuki Yamashita, had a force of some 350,000 men in the Philippines and despite his great numerical superiority (the U.S. troops numbered only 68,000), he was unable to hold back the U.S. advance. It was a turn of events from what had happened four years before. By January 20, U.S. forces had penetrated forty miles inland. Nine days later elements of the U.S. Eighth Army landed near San Antonio on the west coast, while a third landing was made at Nasugbu on January 31. Manila was entered on February 3rd. Assisted by a parachute company that landed near the prison camp at Bilibid, a special task force liberated the prisoners and then continued to mop up the enemy troops...HS

I was standing in the courtyard at Bilibid Prison, about twenty feet from a window covered with boards, when the wood from the window came crashing into the courtyard. Instantly rifle muzzles poked through the window, ready to fire. I started to yell. Three helmeted soldiers came darting through the opening, and at first I thought they were Japanese. I hadn't recognized the helmets, or the uniforms. Still, no mistaking them, they were American G.I.s, and there they stood, an American patrol, ready to shoot us. They were the first Americans we had seen since our capture. They also at first thought we were Japanese.

When they saw we were prisoners, they lowered their rifles. They had a look on their faces as though they were watching a horror movie. We hastily gathered around them, inspecting their uniforms, their helmets, their rifles. They didn't look anything like the soldiers we were when

American rifleman passes dead Japanese sniper in Manila.

the war broke out, and to them we must have looked pretty pathetic in our tattered rags. We were thin as skeletons, with hollowed cheeks and sunken eyes, our stomachs puffed out, our legs swollen around the knees, and we were riddled with scurvy, beriberi, yellow jaundice and God knows what else. Many of us were so weak it was all we could do to stand. And we jabbered like fools. But we were able to caution them that our Japanese guards were still in the prison. After a few moments they told us to stay put and continued their patrol. We were now more confused than ever. We still didn't know what to expect next.

Our officers who understood Japanese did their best to reason with the Japanese, to try to make them understand that their situation was hopeless and that it was best for them to surrender. They refused to listen. Instead, they put on their best uniforms and with sabres at ready they marched in formation through the main gate. They were met by a volley of machine gun fire from the tanks lined up in front of the prison, and there they died, for their emperor.

Sporadic fighting continued the rest of the day, and just before dark, an American army unit entered the main gate and took up positions in the courtyard. None of us slept again that night. By daylight the prison was filled with well armed American G.I.s.

By now, the Japanese army was retreating toward Intramuros, the Walled City in the old Spanish section of Manila that I had come to know before the war. Intramuros was fairly close to Bilibid Prison. House-to-house fighting raged through the streets and we could hear small arms fire. Once inside Intramuros, the Japanese laid down a mortar barrage and their shells began to drop on the prison. The American command decided to move us quickly.

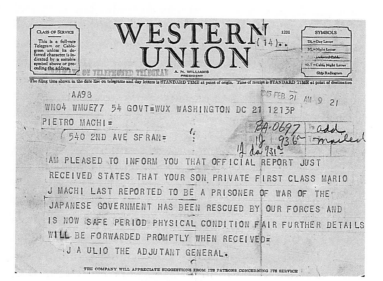

Mario's cable to parents.

Weak and unable to help ourselves, they loaded us into trucks and took us to the abandoned Marikina shoe factory where we remained all night. The next morning they returned us to Bilibid which was probably safer for us than the shoe factory. At least at Bilibid we had thick walls for protection. Outside those walls the battle continued in full fury. That evening the American artillery positioned itself facing Intramuros. We knew at once the sound of our 240mm Howitzers when they opened up. Never had I heard such a barrage! The ground shook beneath us like jello, and talking was impossible. Even when we shouted we couldn't be heard. There was no letup. The barrages at Abucay and Mount Samat had been child's play compared to what was taking place now.

The battle for Manila raged all that day; soon the entire city was on fire. Every building became an inferno. The Japanese were trapped within Intramuros and it was only a matter of time before it was over for them.

During the bombings and artillery barrages on Bataan, I had what I thought was good control of myself, but all this changed during the battle of Manila. For some unknown reason this battle shattered my nerves. I couldn't eat; I couldn't sleep; I couldn't even sit still. I was at the end of my rope and feared I had reached the limit of my endurance. I tried again and again to assure myself that everything would be over in a short time, that the Japanese would surrender and we would be safe, but still, the strain was almost unbearable. I found little comfort in the fact that most of my friends felt the same way.

Again, I resolved to keep busy. As the battle raged, our medical officers decided to put what records we had left, those which we had kept on milk can labels, in safe keeping, and I helped them. We filled some empty boxes and loaded them on trucks waiting in the courtyard.

The pressure became too great for one medical

Liberated U.S. Prisoners after 3 years in Bilibid.

officer. I was coming down the stairs with the load of cartons when I saw him staggering around the truck as if he was drunk. It was all we could do to calm him down.

A day or so after the records had been packed and were aboard the trucks, I was standing near the main gate, listening to American artillery fire pounding away at Intramuros, when I glanced toward the gate entrance. I was surprised to see a group of riflemen run into the prison and take up positions around the area. I couldn't understand it. The prison was already secure. Moments later the riflemen were followed by a dozen or more photographers. Then to my utter surprise, General Douglas MacArthur strode into Bilibid prison followed by his staff. He said in a clear loud voice for all of us to hear, "I have returned." He spent the next half hour visiting the sick. We all were surprised, and deeply honored by his visit. He kept his promise; he did return.

A young woman, an American Red Cross worker, was with the general's party and she asked whether her brother who had been interned at Cabanatuan was here in Bilibid. No one seemed to know who he was and she couldn't find him. I felt so sorry for this woman; she had come such a long way in anticipation of seeing her brother.

On February 4, 1945, all the American prisoners who were in Bilibid, except those unable to travel, boarded transport planes and headed south. It was pleasant just to sit and look down on Bilibid as we flew overhead. What a nightmare the last three years had been! The war had still not been won but our fighter planes seemed to be everywhere, apparently now in complete control of the air. What a change had taken place in our lives in just a few short days.

We bumped down at the airport in Leyte where our American troops were preparing to move north into the Cagayan Valley. We moved around among them freely and talked with everyone we could. They were anxious to hear about our experiences, and we wanted any news we could get, about the war, what was happening back home, who had won the World Series, anything.

Wrecked Quezon Bridge frames devastated Manila.

The shambles that was Manila - 12 Feb 1945.

Chapter 24

HOMEWARD BOUND

———◆◆◆———

The U.S. drive into the Cagayan Valley ended the last offensive on Luzon in June 1945, but enemy pockets of resistance were not cleared out until August 15, when hostilities officially ended. The U.S. forces had officially reported 40,565 casualties including 7,933 killed in the Philippine campaign. The Japanese lost over 192,000 killed and approximately 9,700 captured. An untold number of Japanese soldiers escaped into the jungles of Mindanao in the south and refused to surrender for years to come...HS

At last we boarded *USS Monterey*, a converted luxury liner turned troop transport, that would take us home, with a stopover in New Guinea. I found it too good to believe. After all the humiliation, pain, suffering, and death, we were alive. What a relief just to be treated like human beings, and to be with fellow Americans again.

We were assigned our bunks and shown the showers. These simple pleasures were ultimate luxuries to us. A hot shower, without the need to dip water with a canteen cup, and bars of soap. And a regulation ship's bunk, with mattress and sheets. After showers and clean clothes, we were led to the ship's mess hall where we were allowed to order anything we wanted to eat. My first order was a steak.

We were permitted to go ashore at Hollandia, General MacArthur's headquarters. The port had been the staging area for the offensive war against the Japanese. Everywhere we turned there were troops, equipment, and the knowledge that the Japanese were on the run. Morale was high among the troops.

Once the *Monterey* was back at sea, we headed homeward. The captain pointed the ship's bow straight for San Francisco. Not one man complained as we sailed past Hawaii without stopping. This time we didn't grumble about not having shore leave. We were headed home as quickly as our ship could take us.

We entered the Golden Gate thirteen days after leaving New Guinea. Factory whistles, boat and fog horns, sirens—all announced our arrival and welcomed us home. What a beautiful sight that bridge was, in spite of the fog and drizzle! As the tugs gently pushed *Monterey* toward the pier, I climbed to the upper deck where I could be by myself. I looked anxiously down at the crowd gathered around on the dock to see if I could recognize some of my family. I then saw them, standing on the dock, waving, calling my name. I couldn't hold back the flood of tears.

I quote here from an article written by Bonnie Percival. It appeared in the *San Francisco Chronicle* on Friday, March 16, 1945, the day after our arrival, under the title "Reunion on the Dock." It read:

"The Machi family (ten Strong) cried 'Mario' as the transport came in.

"A giant grey one-time luxury liner crept slowly through the drizzle to a crowded pier on the Embarcadero yesterday morning.

"It was raining...Nobody cared...It was cold...The crowd ignored it. Instead of shivers, there were cries of excitement, anticipation, and happiness from the waiting families of men and women who were captives no longer.

"The delirium was infectious. As the ship grew closer, the row of faces along each deck became recognizable, and waiting relatives began to shout for their returning loved ones.

"The Machi family of 540 second Avenue began it. They had arrived ten strong to greet their brother, son, uncle and nephew...Private first class Mario Machi, thirty-year-old infantryman. He'd spent three years in Camp

Number One and Bilibid. "Mario" shouted his exuberant sister, Catherine Machi. "Mario" echoed another sister, Antonette Machi. "Mario" chorused little Anna Maria and John Papagni, watching for the uncle whose face they could not quite remember.

"The chant for Mario was taken up by the family, by members of British Red Cross, by others of the crowd until a dark lean soldier climbed up on a netted life raft and waved eagerly back."

I was home again. Thank God I was back. I was alive. Who could ever possibly understand this more than the men who had endured those dreadful three years in prison with me? Yet we could not speak of it, not then.

We were driven by bus to Letterman General Hospital, the site of my enlistment, and the next day the city of San Francisco held a grand parade down Market Street in our honor. That evening it was my father's turn. He prepared a gala spaghetti dinner at our home, and twenty-one of my buddies from prison camp attended. It was moments like this we had dreamed about for the past three years. And my father was the proudest man in San Francisco.

From Letterman I was transferred as a patient to Dibble General Hospital in Menlo Park, followed by a stay at Mitchell Convalescent Hospital in San Diego. World War II officially came to an end at 9:04 a.m. on September 2, 1945 when the Japanese Foreign Minister Mamoru Shigemitsu and military leaders signed the formal surrender documents on board the battleship *USS Missouri*, anchored in Tokyo Bay. A few weeks later on September 15, 1945, I received my honorable discharge at Mitchell. I rode the night train from Los Angeles to San Francisco. A new life was about to begin.

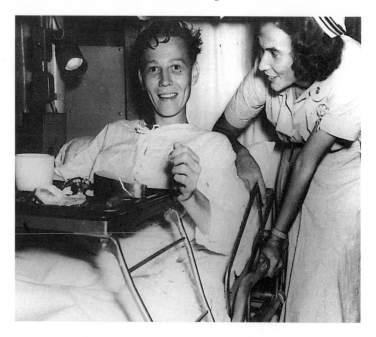

Happy with his first meal in a long time.

Chapter 25

SUMMING UP

———◆——

At Letterman Hospital before my discharge I was happy to meet with many of those who had survived with me the Death March and nearly three years of prison. It was great to see old friends again and spend time with them. We watched film of other prisoners of war being released from camps in the Philippines. Many faces I recognized, some that I had worked with, appeared on the screen. One face took me by complete surprise. It was the navy chief, the one with all the tattoos and the two word vocabulary, the man from Cabanatuan who wouldn't give up. There he was, keeping up with the rest of the men, stepping down the road with his right leg, dragging his left. He had made it back to States!

Another prisoner who had miraculously survived the Death Ward at Camp Cabanatuan and made it back to the States was the man who had requested a pinch of salt. With the salt he had recovered sufficiently to work on the farm, but his first day proved to be too hard for him and they carried him back on a stretcher. He then contracted tuberculosis and they carried him to the T.B. ward. I now learned he had spent the remainder of his internment in the ward from where he was liberated. I don't know where he is now, but I would be willing to wager he could be found alive somewhere.

One day shortly before I checked out of Letterman, we were told to dress up in our best uniform and put on our finest smiles. General Joseph Stilwell was coming to pay us a visit. We all had a great admiration for General Stilwell, or "old Vinegar Joe," as his troops called him. He had fought the Japanese in China and Burma throughout the war. He had marched with the remnants of his defeated army across Burma to India, some 140 miles, with the Japanese close behind them. He was a hero to all of us.

I put on my new uniform, now with corporal chevrons, and stepped outside. The surprise came when General Stilwell awarded me the Bronze Star for the work I had done with the sick and disabled prisoners in the camps.

After the war the U.S. Military conducted war crime hearings in Manila. Among the accused was the Japanese commander of the invasion forces in the Philippines, Lieutenant General Homma Masaharu. He was charged with responsibility for the Death March and was tried by an U.S. military commission in Manila in January-February 1946. Convicted of war crimes, he was executed on April 3rd the same year.

Almost a year after the war ended, I was completing my studies in San Francisco when a small parcel arrived at my home. It was from the Philippines. I quickly opened it, trying hard to imagine what might be inside. I undid the final wrapping, and there neatly tied was a small note book. It was my diary, the one I had given to a Filipino man during the death march, a man I had never seen before. His name was Juan Evangelista and he had made the following addition to my diary:

"April 20, 1942. Monday (11:30AM)

"While I was searching for my brother (who has graduate a High School and trained for month Cadre and when the World War II broke out he was commissioned as Sergeant of the USAFFE (PA) 31st Eng Co. C at the age of less than 18 years), When a group of Americans are at rest while I was at a window of a native house. We have served a little of what we have and it happened that Mr.

Mario Machi approached me and handed his 2 note books as diaries and photographs he has requested me to keep them. (I was at San Pedro _____ where we meet each other.) "

Tears filled my eyes, and I could remember the very moment I handed him my diaries. How I wanted to see him again, to thank him, to tell him I was alive, but there was no address.

I have kept up over the years with a few friends from camp. John "Red" Bohn, a navy man I first met in Letterman hospital now lives in Santa Rosa, California. We were in different outfits but got together now and then in camp. He appeared often in my diary and was one of the men I had climbed the summit with that October 3, 1941, while we were still at Fort McDowell.

Arthur McBain is another old friend from Bataan. He was a navy corpsman who married a Filipina after the war. He and his wife live in Morgan Hill, California. We occasionally visit one another. Many of the photographs that appear in this book came from his collection.

My story does not end here. There was something I still had to do.

Chapter 26

RETURN TO BATAAN

———◆———

Wreath-laying is a year-round affair and a deeply ingrained custom in the Philippines, but the most important and lengthiest speeches that accompany these ceremonies are reserved for April 9, the date of Bataan's fall. On that day, the President of the Philippines is the one who usually leads a throng of ex-heroes up Mount Samat, site of the fiercest battle in 1942 before the Filipino American forces capitulated. At the summit stands a great 300-foot cross marking a memorial shrine to the war dead, known as Dambana ng Kagitingan, the Shrine of Valor. The shrine at any time of the year is a popular tourist spot...HS

On April 5, 1980, a group of aging, gray-haired men and women gathered at the San Francisco International Airport and prepared to travel to the Philippine Islands. They were returning to Bataan. I was among them.

We represented all major service branches—army, navy, air force, marines, nurses and more—and we all shared a common experience. We had been prisoners of war, hostages of the Emperor of Japan, during World War II. Some were accompanied by their families. I was with my wife Shirley and my two daughters, Toni and Gina.

The decision to return to Bataan and relive the death march in which so many friends had died did not come easy. When I returned to the States in 1945 I decided that the only way to carry on a normal existence was to shut out my war experiences and concentrate on the present. For thirty-five years, with a few exceptions, I thought I had done so. I had forced from my mind those memories that could have haunted and disturbed me. Whether my experiences had been completely forgotten

170

or whether they were still in my subconsciousness seemed unimportant.

It was curiosity more than anything else that drew me back to the Philippines. I had a deep affection for the Filipinos, and I wanted to visit their country once more and see what changes had taken place since the war's end. I also thought the experience would be good for my daughters, who at that time were teenagers. So we joined a tour organized for prisoners of war and their families.

I failed to recognize anyone in the group, but after sharing experiences we discovered that most of us had been in the same camps at about the same time. We could even recall some Japanese guards and many incidents.

The theme of our excursion was "Reunion for Peace" and it was to include a group of Japanese soldiers who had served in the Japanese army during the battle on Mt. Samat, our last battle ground in April of 1942. I had misgivings as to the success of our first meeting with the Japanese, since I feared that some men in our group still held grudges. They had seen too many American soldiers perish from starvation, disease, and brutal treatment in the prison camps.

Although we stayed at the same hotels, there was little fraternization between the Japanese and Americans. On one occasion, at a roadside restaurant, we came upon fifty of the Japanese soldiers already seated. They applauded our group for about five minutes, but some Americans would not enter the restaurant because of their presence. I think "Reunion for Peace" was a great idea, but I also think that it will take a few more years to heal the wounds inflicted by those prison-camp experiences. To some the wound will never heal.

When we arrived at Manila, we did not find the same city we had left the day our army captured Bilibid Prison and set us free. Manila that day was devastated and burning. Today it's a modern, beautiful city with high rises, gardens and grand vistas. The city has changed, but the Filipinos have not. They were just as warm and receptive as when I knew them before and during the war. What excitement to return!

Veteran groups, women's auxiliaries, and civic groups were on hand to welcome us. A military band played the Philippine national anthem and "The Star-Spangled Banner." There were a few short welcoming speeches at the airport. Shaking hands with the Filipino soldiers was a very emotional experience for me.

The next morning we visited the Tomb of the Unknown Soldiers. William Montgomery, a former officer who fought with the Filipinos on Bataan, placed a wreath at the site. This man's legs were deformed and he was almost blind as a result of the malnutrition and beriberi he suffered as a prisoner of war. In spite of his condition, he climbed up and down stairs throughout our excursions with a smile on his face.

Our next stop was the Manila Cemetery, situated at Fort Bonifacio. I had been stationed there briefly in 1941 when it was Fort William McKinley. The cemetery is in a dramatic setting. The entrance is located at the far side of a large grass circle. Immediately beyond the entrance is a plaza with a circular fountain. To the right of the fountain is the visitors' building and, stretching from the plaza to the memorial, is the central mall.

I stood before this beautiful and majestic memorial and my thoughts returned to my internment days in Camp O'Donnell, Cabanatuan, and Bilibid. I visualized the suffering in those dreadful days. I remembered how we made an effort to identify our dead by placing metal name tags in their mouths when we buried them in the common graves, hoping that someday they could have a decent burial. Now, the names of these men of Bataan are inscribed in marble. Thank God, at least here they had not been forgotten.

Tears came to my eyes as I tried to express my gratitude silently to the United States and Philippine governments and to all those involved in creating this memorial. Thirty-five years seemed like a moment in my life as images raced with lightning speed through my mind and the memories seemed to fade away and I found myself in Manila again at the beginning of World War II.

From Manila we returned to Bataan. The whole nightmare that I thought had been over for thirty-five years was now in front of me.

I watched General Hipps, a member of our party, place a wreath on the Tomb of the Unknown Soldier, and we then continued our journey over the very same route we had tread on the death march in 1942. Each kilometer was marked with a signpost, and each mark brought back a memory.

That afternoon we arrived at the Kamaya Point Hilltop Hotel at Mariveles. My family and I retired to our rooms and, as we drew the curtain to see the view, the island of Corregidor, scarcely five miles from the hotel, stood framed in our window. A breathtaking view, but what memories it evoked! I could almost see the sky lighted with the red glow of heavy gun fire, and I could smell the smoke. In my mind I was standing next to the truck, with the squat little Japanese soldier behind the wheel, trying to stretch his legs to reach the pedals. I hadn't remembered him in all those years. And there were other thoughts that came to mind, and other faces from the past that appeared before me. My wife and daughters somehow knew the anguish I was going through, and my wife placed a hand on my shoulder. I could not escape the past, but I could be thankful for what I had now.

The Ninth of April is designated a national holiday

in the Philippines. It's known as Bataan Day and commemorates the anniversary of the surrender on Bataan. Our destination was Mount Samat. On our way to the mountain, we could see a huge cross on its crest. It can easily be seen for thirty kilometers. This magnificent cross is a memorial to those servicemen and women who fought to hold back the Japanese. For generations to come, it will remind others of the battle that took place on these slopes.

As we approached the area near the foot of the cross, we were greeted by people from various veterans' organizations and quite a gathering of Filipinos. Philippine Army troops stood at attention as a plaque was unveiled honoring the Angels of Bataan, the nurses who had served on Bataan and had been interned at Santo Tomas in Manila.

As I gazed at the memorial, I was again surprised at how clearly I remembered the chaos of those days and the inhuman hardships we endured from the Japanese. And it was at this time that I began thinking about writing my experiences in a book.

The next day, we boarded two banka boats for the trip to Corregidor. They were narrow boats equipped with outriggers to balance and help keep them steady.

Forty-five minutes later we landed on the island, boarded buses and toured the historical army outpost. We visited the Malinta Tunnel and saw General MacArthur's headquarters, the hospital area, and other areas of interest. I went topside and wandered around the gun emplacements. These huge naval guns had been originally set to fire on any attack from the sea and were unable to fire inland toward Bataan. After looking at the big guns, I had the feeling that we might have been able to defend the Philippines if only they could have given us cover on Bataan. Some men standing by my side talked about their frustrations in defending Corregidor, and they pointed to battle stations where they were involved in firing the guns during the battle of Corregidor.

That evening in Manila we attended a party hosted by General Santos at his residence, and when we returned to our hotel rooms we found our sheets turned back and floral arrangements on our pillows. The gesture deeply moved me. I couldn't help thinking about Camp O'Donnell!

On the fourteen of April, we boarded our buses for Baguio, the summer capital of the Philippines. On our way we stopped briefly at Clark Field, the American air base, and then proceeded to Camp O'Donnell, the prisoner of war camp where over 1500 American men and about 5000 Filipino soldiers had died after coming off the death march. The original buildings were gone, but we visited a death march memorial.

At the picturesque mountain city of Baguio, we were greeted at Sunshine Park by Mayor Bueno. At sixteen years of age, he had fought with guerrillas during World War II. He had also served in Korea and Vietnam and presently held the rank of brigadier general. President Marcos had appointed him mayor of Baguio.

During our three-day stay in Baguio, we visited Camp John Hay, now a rest and recreational area for American Servicemen. This was where General Tomoyuki Yamashita, the tiger of Malaya, signed the surrender papers, ending the war in the Philippines. We also visited the United States ambassador's residence, toured the Philippine Military Academy at Fort del Pilar and on April seventeenth we left Baguio via Lingayen Gulf where, in 1945, American soldiers stormed ashore with tanks and raced to Manila to free us from Bilibid prison.

The night before we boarded our planes for San Francisco, we were guests of Mayor Ramon Bagatsing of

Manila. The highlight of evening was the presentation of the Philippine Defense and Liberation Medals to veterans of Bataan and a special ceremony honoring the nurses.

The next day we were on our way back to San Francisco. My Bataan experience had come full circle, though with a difference. Before it had been necessary to forget, now it was important to remember, to think it through, to write it down.